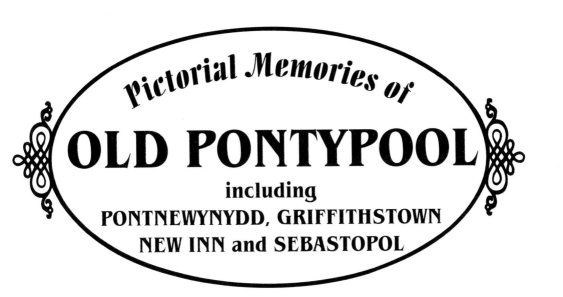

Pictorial Memories of
OLD PONTYPOOL
including
PONTNEWYNYDD, GRIFFITHSTOWN
NEW INN and SEBASTOPOL

by Bryan Roden

Foreword by
Yvonne Warren
Mayor of Torfaen 2004

Volume 3

Old Bakehouse Publications

Abertillery

© Bryan Roden

First published in October 2004

ISBN 1 874538 38 7

Published in the U.K. by
Old Bakehouse Publications
Church Street,
Abertillery, Gwent NP13 1EA
Telephone: 01495 212600 Fax: 01495 216222
Email: oldbakehouseprint@btopenworld.com

Made and printed in the UK
by J.R. Davies (Printers) Ltd.

British Library Cataloguing in Publication Data: a catalogue
record for this book is available from the British Library.

Foreword
by Yvonne Warren
Mayor of Torfaen 2004

I have to say that I consider it both an honour and pleasure to be invited to write the foreword for this wonderful book - Pictorial Memories of Old Pontypool Volume 3 by local author Bryan Roden.

Readers will enjoy and be fascinated by the wealth of material found yet again in this latest edition, the third such publication by Bryan. We are instantly reminded of those wistful words *'a picture can tell a thousand stories'*. And then one wonders just how many stories might actually lie within these pages, for the variety is bound to be extremely wide and interesting without doubt. I began by glancing through the contents, not putting it down until several hours later, only to pick it up again the following day, such was my enthusiasm.

I know that you will agree how fortunate we are to have such people as Bryan Roden within our community who research so thoroughly and diligently to produce what amounts to a comprehensive historic legacy. Our present generation, and those that are destined to follow in our footsteps in the years ahead within the boundaries of Pontypool, do and hopefully will continue to appreciate the enormous value of books such as this.

I commend it to everyone, please enjoy and preserve!

Yvonne Warren

Contents

Introduction

It was in 1998 that the first volume of this series of Pontypool books first appeared, followed by Volume Two in 2000 and now in 2004 I have yielded to temptation and produced the third and probably final edition. The remarkable success of the previous books is possibly attributable to an unstinting, modern-thinking population, yet one that does not necessarily wish to let go of the past entirely and still has a desire to do a little reminiscing now and again, without being accused of locking themselves into a time warp and dwelling too much on the past. In the last four years since the publication of Volume 2, much has been going on with particular emphasis being placed on rejuvenating the town as a modern-looking shopping centre for the benefit of everyone. As this book goes to print, any remaining traces of a once-busy railway station for instance are being replaced with a new supermarket and Crane Street is receiving some long-overdue attention, all of which will hopefully brighten up the town, bring a new lease of life and the return of prosperous times. It has to be appreciated by everyone, that in the name of progress, many things will never be the same again and the age-old conversations about the 'good old days' and 'the best years of our lives' will go on forever. There are of course divided opinions here, for some of those 'good old days' were in fact some of the 'worst' in economic terms but the best maybe, in moral terms. Many of the photographs in this book will help illustrate some of those special times, such as the array of shops occupying George Street, Crane Street and Commercial Street but, after looking at picture number 7 for example, with a selection of raw meat for sale and hanging out in the open, one might have second thoughts. Further reminders from this era include the Park Temperance Hotel in Commercial Street which offered a first-class hot dinner for no more than 1/- (5p) whilst a few yards away, half a century later, was a branch of 'The Fifty Shilling Tailor' where a gent's suit could actually be bought for 50 shillings (£2.50 in today's money, and as decimal currency has been with us now for 33 years, those readers who can remember so-called 'real money' are probably getting fewer and fewer). The areas that surround Pontypool are also well-represented photographically with glimpses of a few industrial 'has-beens' such as Pontnewynydd Forge, the hammers of which have not sounded aloud for more than forty years, whilst in more recent times, steelmaking at Panteg Works has come to an end after more than 100 years, leaving Griffithstown and Sebastopol far quieter places in the 21st century.

The concluding chapter offers a small selection of scenes of past and present Pontypool, which in my previous books have attracted much interest, providing perfect examples of continuing changes that go on around us, often without realising their importance. I extend my warm thanks to all those who have purchased the preceding volumes and trust that this publication will be greeted with the same enthusiasm which I find so encouraging.

Bryan Roden

CHAPTER 1

Pontypool Town and its Traders

1. One of Pontypool's popular hotels from years past, 'Walker's Waverley' situated in Crane Street. Dated 1891 and pictured some fifteen years later, the hotel's proprietor was Mr. John Walker whose other enterprise 'The Victoria Coffee Tavern' was positioned lower down the street. The 'Waverley', advertised as the most comfortable temperance hotel in South Wales, catered specially for commercial gentlemen and parties. As well as being a hotel, this spacious building also comprised of a restaurant known as 'The Albert' and a 'Little Gem' confectionery shop.

2. The 'town end' of Osborne Road and a period scene from the middle of the Edwardian decade. The horse and trap stands outside Pontypool's main post office, while next door a bicycle is seen in the doorway of the Army Recruitment Office. The nearest shop premises, now the site of the town's down-graded post office, is that of hairdresser and tobacconist George Roach. Some readers will recall the building in later years when occupied by 'Masters Clothiers'.

3. The junction of Osborne Road and George Street in the 1950s, which today's younger generation may have some difficulty in pin-pointing the exact location. Facing the camera, the business premises occupied at the time by window-cleaning contractors Palmer and Sons, tailors and outfitters Williams & Jones and Williams Brothers, dealers in cycles, toys and baby carriages all vanished in the following decade, during the demolition of 1963.

4. Crane Street from The Cross in 1906, the scene captured by local photographer Mr. T.A. Jones on a seemingly quiet morning. The bay window nearest left formed part of Fowlers store and one door further on, stands Woods the chemist as seen in the picture below. Almost sixty-five years were to pass before the loss of the buildings at the upper part of the street was to commence, thus changing its appearance forever.

5. Located at Number 1 Crane Street in the early years of the twentieth century was pharmaceutical chemist and druggist Godfrey Charles Wood. Mr. Wood who started in the town as a chemist in 1893 at the above site, expanded the business in the following decade when he opened another store, combining as a tobacconist at Number 5 George Street. Besides trading for more than 35 years, Mr. Wood also served as a church chorister for 55 years and a church warden at Trevethin for seven.

6. Commercial Street in the year 1903 with the central building of the London & Provincial Bank dominating the scene. The George Hotel and Fowlers store are visible to the left, while opposite, the advertising sign behind the lamppost is that of Croom & Son, tailors and hosiers at Number 15. The drug store nearest at Number 23 belonged to the Roderick brothers where, in 1872 over thirty years previous, an iron oven thought to have once been used by the Allgood family in the manufacture of Japan Ware was being used as a water butt at the rear of the shop.

7. A fine display of carcasses hangs outside Eastmans the butcher during the early years of the last century. As well as this shop at Number 25 Commercial Street, which was managed by Mr. Arthur Abbot, the company also ran a stall in the Market Hall. Besides Eastmans, Pontypool had an abundance of butchery tradesmen, boasting of over thirty locations in and around the town of which almost two-thirds were to be found in the town's market.

8. An impressive view of George Street dating from about 1910. Amongst the familiar shop signs are the premises of wine and spirit merchants W. & A. Gilbey's, sited behind the gentleman stood with the horse, the board above advertising Rogers Ales & Stouts. The Bristol brewery of W.J. Rogers was taken over in 1935 by Simonds of Reading and was one of a number of English-based brewers who at the time, were active in South Wales and Monmouthshire capturing their share of this very competitive market.

9. Moving onwards to the early 1930s with another exceptional view of George Street this time from the opposite direction and turning into Osborne Road is one of the district's early motor buses. It was in the previous decade of the 1920s that keen rivalry existed between the local firm Barretts (Eastern Valley Motor Services) and Messrs Ralphs of Abertillery, who were competing for increasing passenger business in the Pontypool district. This rivalry often resulted in bus drivers racing against each other but was brought to a sudden halt in 1930 with the introduction of the Road Traffic Act, intent on curbing such dangerous practices on the country's highways. The Tobacco Box, a shop seen on the left, was in earlier years the site of the National Provincial Bank and later a branch of the Quality Cleaners occupied the premises.

10. The former Castle Brewery positioned at the rear of the Castle Hotel in George Street and viewed shortly before its demolition. Founded in the 1830s, the brewery flourished throughout many years and continued to do so until the company, along with its nine public houses was taken over by Westlakes Brewery of Cwmavon during the second decade of the twentieth century. Subsequently, in July 1933, the Westlakes pubs were incorporated into a new company registered in the name of The Reform Brewery of Abersychan. By 1939 however, even this newly-formed company was the subject of a successful takeover bid from a larger operation, that of Andrew Buchan's Brewery of Rhymney which went on to become one of Wales's foremost beer producers, Rhymney Breweries Limited.

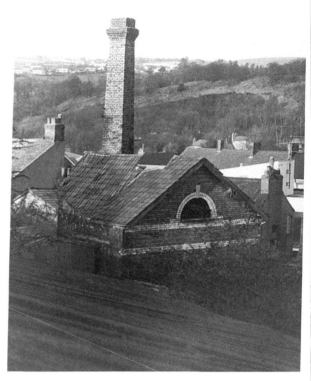

11. Before the complete destruction and widening of George Street, redevelopment had already begun a little earlier with the construction of a new supermarket 'Fine Fare' as seen here. Photographed in 1966 and now occupied by a 'Kwik Save' store, adjacent to a branch of Boots the Chemist, the area has become the busiest part of town, if somewhat lacking the character of the old street.

12./13. Two further scenes of old George Street from the 1960s with all of the buildings on the left-hand side having since been demolished. Both views are facing towards The Cross and epitomise the traffic problems at the time and the ensuing danger to pedestrians despite a number of plans being submitted to provide a solution. Sometime between the two world wars the council proposed knocking down one side of the street and completely re-building it further back, a plan that failed to materialize due to protests from some council members and traders that rates would have to rise significantly to fund it. A subsequent plan, which was also rejected due to high costs, was to build a bypass behind George Street from the Post Office to Barclays Bank. A more ambitious project was to build a road through the park but opponents quickly pointed out that this would seriously divert trade away from the town and spoil the park's splendour forever. The debate on what to do about George Street dragged on until 1957 when the council finally decided that it had no choice but to do something quite positive. The usual disagreements persisted until eventually, with the aid of a grant from the Ministry of Transport, work began on July 10th 1963.

14. Unrecognisable today, this particular photograph dating from the 1950s provides an opportunity to look down the lower part of High Street. Once a busy thoroughfare with a thriving collection of almost thirty businesses, the street is now just a shadow of its former self and sadly all of the buildings seen above have disappeared. On the immediate right is the old town school that is also featured in a later chapter of this book.

15. Looking in the opposite direction of the photograph above, this view dating from over a decade ago, has been transformed completely by the construction of Pontypool's by-pass and the only buildings remaining are the blocks of flats at the top end. The former town school was positioned just below the flats and the structure nearest, with its prominent chimney stack, would have been located to the left of the previous picture.

16. Moving on further up High Street and a view from the late 1960s or early 1970s is recalled. The scene was photographed near a spot once occupied by one of the town's devotional structures erected in the 1850s - the Wesleyan Methodist Chapel. Nearest, the derelict Rehoboth Welsh Calvinistic Church along with some former business premises are in sight, as are those that appear in Picture 14 situated on the extreme right at the bottom of the street.

17. Sandbrook and Dawe which was virtually an 'institution' in the town from 1817 until its demise in 1989, is seen here during its 'Closing-Down Sale' in the wake of approaching demolition. Some fifteen years have passed since this hardware store was concluded and whilst such a long-serving trader as this might never again appear in Pontypool, hopefully the redevelopment of Crane Street has attracted some new businesses to serve the town's shoppers for years to come.

18. The Park Temperance Hotel & Restaurant, an impressive building in Commercial Street. Just above the doorway on the right, the name of S. Osborne is advertised as the proprietor who in these Edwardian times offered 'good substantial hot dinners at 6d, 9d and 1/- '. (at $2^1/_2$p, 4p and 5p respectively, these were good days to dine out in Pontypool). The name Osborne also appeared amongst other ventures in the town during this period that may well have been family-associated such as, Edwin Osborne whose refreshment rooms were situated in High Street and a Thomas Osborne in Crane Street who was listed as a 'hard confectioner'.

19. Two of the district's law-enforcers are featured in this Edwardian view of Commercial Street. The constable walking on the pavement and wearing a 'bush hat' policed in the Abersychan area. This particular headgear was adopted from soldiers returning from the Boer War at the turn of the twentieth century, but was not so successful in coping with weather conditions of the Gwent valleys in comparison to the hot sun of South Africa's veldt; consequently the standard police helmet was soon put back into use.

20. A traffic-congested Commercial Street at the junction with Market Street on a sunny day in the 1960s. The structure in the centre with its 1930 facia was at the time occupied by 'The Fifty Shilling Tailor', one of a number of gentlemen's clothing retailers in the town. Times have certainly changed, the paying customer now having to travel further afield than Pontypool to purchase such items.

21. A view from the not too distant past showing the demise of the old police station that adjoined Pontypool's town hall. The station which has since made way for the Borough's new Civic Centre, was for a number of years utilised as offices by the local council. The other building in the foreground, once connected with weights and measures was also demolished soon after.

22. In what might be described as a 'grandstand view', this scene at Crane Street was photographed from the old railway bridge on a busy market day in 1899 with The Globe Hotel on the right evidently offering a useful parking spot for visiting traders. As well as market days, at the time held on Wednesdays and Saturdays, other popular attractions included the fairs. These were well-attended events conducted in February, April (twice), July and October and were described as being for pleasure, horses, sheep and cheese.

23. The years move on in Crane Street to around 1930 and the former Simpson shop has been acquired by Hodges & Sons. On the opposite side of the street, between The Swan Inn and The Three Cranes is the alleyway entrance to Tabernacle Baptist Church once situated behind these two hostelries. Further down the street is a motor car, the first signs that motor traffic is gradually taking over from the horse and trap as the new mode of transport.

24. A 1960's reminder of how Crane Street car park used to look prior to the demolition of the above properties and where the new shopping development is taking hold. Tabernacle Chapel and its Sunday School appear in the right foreground, whilst behind the Sunday School and cottages on the left, the roof of Pontypool's renowned 'Queens Ballroom' is also visible.

25. The well-known and imposing three-storey building of Daniel Wheatley Simpson's store positioned on the corner of Market Street and Crane Street. This shop stocked a wide range of clothing and accessories, with its advertisement of 1906 (the date of this photograph) offering juvenile clothing, hats, caps, umbrellas, hosiery and shirts on the ground floor, woollen, cutting rooms and men's and youths' clothing to be found on the first floor and the top floor reserved for the tailors' workshop and stock rooms.

26. There should be quite a number of readers of this book that will remember the shop building at Number 36 Crane Street when it stood adjacent to The Three Cranes Hotel and opposite The Globe, which still stands today. This particular photograph is from about 1930 when it was a drapery store occupied by a Miss Elizabeth Rowland but, along with the adjoining premises, it was razed to the ground in 1970.

CARDIFF DRAPERY.   E. ROWLAND, Proprietress.

Lle arbennig am Ddillad Plant.

Fancy Draper.

.. Hosier, etc. ..

Infants' Frocks   Children's Woollies
of all kinds   in great variety.

36 Crane Street, PONTYPOOL.
OPPOSITE STATION APPROACH

27. A scene from Upper Trosnant Street during the 1920s where Mrs. Gladys Evans is pictured in the foreground. Mrs. Evans and her husband William Arthur Evans resided in nearby Clarence Street where they ran a motor garage situated between the Clarence Hotel and Carlton Café, the garage in later years to be known as the Clarence Hotel Garage. In more recent years, readers may remember Mr. Jack Bryant and his Pontypool School of Motoring occupying the same site.

28. A rarely-seen view of Park Road as it appeared before the buildings on the right-hand side were pulled down. Those buildings included The Forge Hammer public house, the stores of T.H. Williams and just below, the unforgettable Park Cinema. Behind the stationary car seen lower down, was another established business that is no more in the town, the concern of monumental stonemasons Jones and Son.

29. This is a closer look at the Old Forge Hammer Stores, Park Road, the business of Thomas Hubert Williams as mentioned above. The property was converted from what was the old or lower Forge Hammer pub and opened as a small shop in 1925 and remained as such until 1954, when it was extended for the selling of a wide variety of goods. The name was later changed to 'Gordon Stores' which many readers may find easier to recall, it being taken over by Mr. Williams's son Gordon following his father's death in 1958. Like so many other family businesses in the area, it finally met its fate in 1968.

30./31. The works of monumental stonemason Ken Jones and son Alan as referred to earlier, stood in Park Road and is seen here in the 1960s. The origins of this family firm date back to the 1830s when ancestor Thomas Jones arrived from Yorkshire to establish a building company in Pontypool. After over twenty years as a building contractor he turned to monumental masonry, starting the trade in Albion Road on a site that was, many decades later, to become the Clarence Bus Station. Mr. Jones's son Frederick continued here until 1914 when it was decided to move to Park Road where it remained until the enforced closure on Ken Jones through road development in January 1976. It is however, one family business that has survived it all, with Mr. Alan Jones still continuing this highly skilled trade to this day at the workshop in Commercial Street, Griffithstown. The picture below is of the original Albion Road site with founder's son Frederick Jones stood on the left between two monuments.

32. The former Trosnant Lodge once situated in Clarence Street opposite the Clarence Hotel. Amongst the occupants of this Victorian structure over the years were Dr. Bertram Siddons and Dr. Enid Mary Siddons who moved here from Osborne Road in about 1930, and whose surgery is seen on the right of the house. Their son Michael carried on in the practice with Dr. Coleman until the latter part of the 1960s when, with his French lady wife, Dr. Michael Siddons emigrated to Canada. This resulted in closure of the practice with patients then transferring to Park Terrace surgery.

33. Making its way out of town during the 1950s, a Ford Thames bus belonging to local firm Peakes of Pontnewynydd turns into Clarence Street. The premises on the corner with Trosnant Street advertising Bevan's Furnishers, had various usages during its lifetime before demolition. These included an Indian restaurant, a carpet shop and pool hall. Nowadays, the site is occupied by a number of flats collectively known as Trosnant Villa.

34. A view overlooking Clarence Corner from a position behind Clarence Street Station in 1914. On the extreme right of centre stands the Carlton Café and Steam Bakery of Edward Stanley Furlow, whose father John founded the family business in Pontypool in the year 1860. Another trade to note is that of Thomas Williams and Sons, coal, timber, slate and building merchant in what was the old goods shed, sited above the advertising hoarding in the centre of the picture. Park Terrace Primitive Methodist Church is also to be seen in the background. This landmark was finally demolished in 1983.

35. A busy scene during the year of the Suez crisis in 1956 with the filling station and garage belonging to Norman Jenkins at Clarence Corner being besieged by motorists queuing for their fuel ration. This was the first such situation for motorists since the end of the war in 1945 but the biggest shock of all was probably the fact that for the emergency period, petrol prices shot up from 20 pence a gallon to 30 pence overnight!

36./37. Two further views from the 1950s and '60s depicting the business of motor engineer Norman Jenkins. This family company started in 1911 when Norman's father Arthur began manufacturing and repairing bicycles in premises where Clarence Chambers now stand. In the photograph above, Norman, the shorter of the two gentlemen on the right, stands outside the garage he himself had built after taking over from his father in the late 1930s. Around 1950 the business expanded when Norman bought the petrol station and garage from Mr. Bob Warman shown in picture 35. Also included was the house shown below, known as Weighbridge House, so-named after the weighbridge positioned a short distance out of the picture to the left. The house was used by the family until 1965 when due to ill-health, Norman sold both garages to the Esso company who demolished the house soon after. Norman's son Richard continued the family business at the rear of the Clarence Hotel until January 1979, when it was decided to move to a site in Rockhill Road, where it remained until closure in December 1999. Richard however, although ending the long relationship with Pontypool after almost ninety years, retained the family interests in the motor trade at Abergavenny until enforced closure through a sudden compulsory purchase order in respect of major road upgrading, took place in mid 2004. Norman Jenkins who emigrated with his wife Maud to Australia in 1978 sadly passed away there in January 2004 at the grand age of 95.

CHAPTER 2

The Surrounding Area

38. The period for the above view looking up Trosnant Street is the 1940s, a few years after the end of World War Two. As will be noted, these ancient dwellings were by now, falling into a state of disrepair with many being condemned for habitation and it was only a matter of time before their removal was to commence.

39. Rockhill Road facing in the direction of Pontymoile Corner and showing the former Education Settlement located on the right which had recently been opened by Chairman of the Pilgrim Trust, Lord Macmillan in June 1937. The Pilgrim Trust was founded in 1930 by American millionaire Stephen Harkness for the benefit of citizens in the United Kingdom and to be used for amongst other things, the preservation of historic buildings, art, learning and social welfare. Now demolished and making way for a new Christian Mission Hall, a 'Settlement' (Community Education Centre) has been established in Trosnant Street, close to Pontypool Leisure Centre.

40. A general view that illustrates part of the district as it appeared in about 1930 seen from the rear of the Clarence Hotel. Clearly visible and located below the housing at Pen-y-Graig Terrace is the approach road to Clarence Street station, one of three such railway stations that once served Pontypool. On the left and in amongst some of the town's older properties is a sign advertising Trumps Auction Rooms whose address at the time was Number 1, Clarence Road. The Trump family were also booksellers in Market Street and later, furniture dealers at 35, Crane Street.

41. As the camera swings left of the previous picture it reveals this snowy scene during the hard winter of 1947 and standing prominently amongst many of the 'now defunct' buildings are the stacks belonging to the former gas works. In the bottom left and facing the camera, is a rare view of some cottages on Mill Road, Trosnant and the author, is grateful to Mr. Brian Jenkins for lending this photograph of where he resided as a young boy.

42. By the mid-1960s it was necessary to start developing Pontymoile's new one-way traffic system and as work is underway, a bus makes it way down Victoria Road on the Upper Race service and heads back towards Pontypool. As may be seen, the tracks of the former Pontypool Road to Neath railway line which closed in 1964, have now been removed. It was during some later improvements to the road system here in 1981 that a number of canal locks were unexpectedly unearthed. These historic remains were part of the Monmouthshire Canal that was constructed by Thomas Dadford Junior and opened in 1796.

43. The first attempt at solving Pontymoile's long-running traffic congestion was not regarded as being very successful, the one-way system soon proving totally inadequate in dealing with the problem. As any motorist or traveller of a few years back will recall, during peak periods, tailbacks as far as St. Hilda's church in Griffithstown and Pontypool Road railway bridge at New Inn, were a common and exasperating experience for all concerned.

44. Another scene at Pontymoile, shortly after the unveiling in November 1910 of a new handsome lamp dedicated to Mr. Alfred Williams, chairman of Panteg Urban District Council, the offices of which are on the right. The corner store to the left once housed the infamous Truck Shop and was occupied during this period by William Jones & Co. who were grocers, bakers and coal merchants. The 1920s saw the Herbert Brothers begin trading here and their shop is seen in the following photograph. Just visible in the distance is a chimney stack that belonged to the Lower Mill Works.

45. The Herbert Brothers' grocers and provision merchants' shop at Fountain Road during the 1960s, having now been trading at the old company Truck Shop premises for more than forty years. During the 18th and 19th centuries the so-called truck system allowed avaricious employers to operate their own shops for their workers, and given a free hand in charging whatever price they felt fit for food and materials, all certainly well above the open market levels. Quite often payment was partly given to employees in company tokens rather than cash, thus forcing them into buying goods at the Truck shop and pouring more profit into the employers' pockets; this practice was eventually abolished with the passing of the Truck Act in 1831. This particular store, which was the last of such illicit establishments in the area to survive as a business proper, is pictured with a smartly-dressed Mr. Herbert outside during the 1960s.

46. A glimpse of what was once part of the Hanbury Farmhouse Bread bakery at Pontymoile in about 1905 with staff operating some of the machinery used in the process. Besides home-grown produce, the flour used for bread-baking here was imported from all over the globe with Canada, Argentina, Russia and Australia having their share in the supply. Today, there is no evidence whatsoever of this former landmark, all having been destroyed by road improvement excavations undertaken in 1981.

47. Yet another former landmark in the district was the Turnpike House at the junction of Usk Road and The Highway pictured here in the early 1960s. As the population became more mobile through the use of horse and carriage, lack of decent road systems soon became apparent. With smaller parishes being unable to finance and maintain such roads, it fell to local businessmen to offer their services by way of opening up highways and charging for the use thereof. The first such experiment began in the early 1700s with the setting up of a Turnpike Trust, a body that would be responsible for a particular road and provide steady revenues for its owners. The idea soon spread and the Pontypool Trust was set up in 1767 and remained as a going concern until 1875, when the local authorities assumed highways control and the building seen above was sold off as a private dwelling.

48. Excluding the young lady with a vintage perambulator, this scene at Crumlin Road appears to have changed very little since portrayed in 1915. A growth of trees on the immediate left stand in the grounds of 'The Wern', while a little distance down the road, is the entrance to Waun Wern House, occupied at the time by industrialist and J.P. Mr. John Paton. Mr. Paton had connections with a number of collieries and works in the vicinity and his former dwelling is no more, the site nowadays being occupied by a mobile-home park.

49. A far-reaching view overlooking the Cwmynyscoy, Blaendare and Race areas, a district of Pontypool that has a long history of industrial heritage. The latest addition to the scenery when photographed in the 1960s was Pontypool College which opened in 1957 and can be seen above the housing of Blaendare Road in the centre of the picture.

50. The houses of Bushy Park, Wainfelin captured almost a century ago. A few years later in November 1911, two of these freehold dwellings appeared for sale by public auction at the Crown Hotel, Pontypool now the location of the Woolworth store. The two houses which at the time were named 'Sainsbury House' and 'Dundas House', were occupied by sitting tenants at a weekly rent of 8/6d and 7/6d (42^{1}/2p and 37^{1}/2p) respectively, with the landlord being responsible for paying the rates and taxes.

51. The most interesting features of this picturesque cottage are probably the shapes and forms of its hedges and shrubs, work known as topiary (the art of trimming and training shrubs and trees into an ornamental fashion). This postcard scene titled 'Yew Tree Cottage Pontypool' was taken in about 1902 by Mr. T.A. Jones whose studio was situated in Park Road. Whilst it has not been possible to ascertain the precise whereabouts of this cottage, the Trevethin area is thought to be a strong contender.

52./53. An idyllic scene depicting an area of Penygarn in the year 1909. The gate entrance right of the large tree leads into the American Gardens and opposite, stands the lodge-keeper's cottage. Known previously as the American Grounds, the gardens were converted in the mid 19th century when ironworks throughout the South Wales valleys were going through a difficult period, causing unemployment and hardship. To provide work for some of the local unemployed, Capel Hanbury Leigh undertook its transformation by developing a lake, laying paths and planting more shrubs and trees, including Californian coniferous trees (sequoias) which were shipped from the Pacific coast of America. To house a caretaker, a rustic lodge which lies a short distance inside the gardens was also constructed. The cottage and lodge both survive to this day and are still inhabited together with a third dwelling known as Tank Cottage. It was the occupants of Tank Cottage who once regulated the sluice gates controlling Nant-y-Gollen stream and the water supply to Park House. The photograph below shows the picturesque gardens as they looked during the 19th century while the developed lake, then a feature of the grounds is now sadly overgrown.

54. Described as 'A peep at Pontypool from Penygarn Road', this view from about 1916 portrays how the steep hill looked before much of the housing development now in place, began to materialize during the following decades.

55. A view overlooking Pontnewynydd which, if photographed from a similar spot today, would reveal the vast amount of changes that have taken place since this 1960s appearance. On close study of Hanbury Road to the right, the scene shows a number of now-defunct buildings while left of centre, the vacant ground and remaining office block leaves a reminder of what was once the site of one of the district's main employers, Pontnewynydd Works, now replaced by an industrial estate.

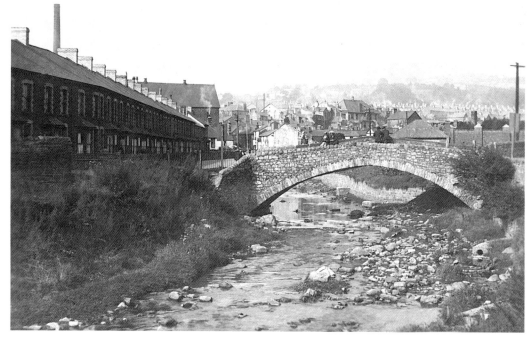

56. Pontnewynydd's ancient stone bridge spanning the Afon Llwyd as viewed from the river's edge in the 1930s. The sturdy houses of Lewis Terrace stand on the left and the once-popular Pavilion Cinema is visible at the far end of the houses. It is said that during the second half of the 19th century, when the river was clean and devoid of colliery waste, baptisms were witnessed by hundreds of onlookers. Converts would walk into the waters and after baptism were taken to nearby dwellings for a change into dry clothing.

57. A familiar occurrence at Hanbury Road, Pontnewynydd during the depression years of the 1930s when groups of unemployed men would be found congregating on street corners with nothing more to do than chat and pray for work. There are a few other such familiar sights from latter days here such as the drinking fountain, which was erected in 1899, a Peake's bus parked outside its depot and on the near left 'Bristol House', one of the district's grocery shops. This business was then in the hands of Mr. Evan W. Evans whose advertisement is to be seen at the bottom of the previous page.

58. Pictured in 1950 still displaying its Stoke-on-Trent registration number where it had previously been in service, a Peake's bus which is on its way to Cwmffrwdoer, picks up some passengers opposite the Pavilion Cinema before attempting the short climb up Hill Street and onwards to its destination. Directly behind the bus is the garage belonging to another bus company, The Western Welsh whose depot closed in 1967 with staff transferring to premises in Cwmbran.

59. Local church members and officials emerge from the Pavilion and congregate to await the start of a traditional Whitsun march probably during the 1920s and the procession is about to be headed by Pontypool Town Silver Band. The Pavilion opened in April 1914 when it offered a variety of entertainments, its first manager being a Mr. Leslie Beaufort; the name of the building was later slightly changed to 'Wests Pavilion' when Mr. Bill West took over as proprietor. Serving as a cinema for many years, declining audiences brought this to an end with the showing of the last film in September 1968. It was reopened as a Bingo Hall for a number of years after that, though always seeming to retain its local nickname of *'The Pavi'*. Now it is just a memory for many, the building having been demolished like the rest of Pontypool's former cinemas.

60./61. Two scenes from Pontnewynydd which are believed to be of what was probably the worst storm ever to have hit the eastern valley of Monmouthshire, when in May 1931, widespread damage was done to many properties in the area. Over the years a regular occurrence on the road seen above took place opposite the Pavilion Garage where, after heavy rain, water would flow from a tunnel that was thought to extend to the old furnace on Crumlin Road which at one time connected up with the workings of Osborne Forge. In April 1993 when excavation of the roadway opened up the tunnel's entrance, large volumes of water were released causing heavy flooding, resulting in closure of the road and traffic diversions. The top stonework of the entrance bore the inscription CHL 1831 (the initials of Capel Hanbury Leigh) and had been visible for many years. Following the excavation and subsequent exploration by local caver Mr. Bill Gascoine, an iron mine, probably dating back some 300 years was discovered extending beneath the Wainfelin and Tranch districts; the date of 1765 was also revealed 400 metres inside the tunnel where it opens out into the mine workings. The scene below is at Mill Road after flood water had subsided leaving a muddy residue from the Afon Llwyd and giving the residents of Lewis Terrace much cleaning up to do.

62. A panoramic view from more than ninety years ago revealing part of the Pontnewynydd district. To the right of the nearest tree is 'Forge Row', once known as 'New Row' whilst further right, locals may recall 'Mount Pleasant Cottages', 'Forgehammer Row' and 'Llanover Row', all now long gone. Directly above and still standing are the houses numbered '46 to 56 Hanbury Road' along with 'Nightingale Terrace' which were previously known as 'Back Row' and 'Ladies Row' respectively. These names all emanated from the 19th century when the area was referred to as Nightingale Village.

CHAPTER 3

Griffithstown, Sebastopol and New Inn

63. Windsor Road, Griffithstown in the early 1900s, the completion of which took place in the final decade of the 19th century when it was built through to join High Street at the far end. On the opposite corner to draper and outfitter F.E. Jenkins, is the steam bakery of Herbert James Thomas who, over the years won a number of awards for his quality products. In one particular competition in 1904, a gold medal with an enormous sum for the time of £100 was won at the bakers' exhibition, an event open to the whole of the country. To celebrate this remarkable achievement, Mr. Thomas gave every child in the local council school a two-penny bun - the school at the time accommodating over 300 pupils!

64. The period is now half a century later and senior citizens of the community will most probably recall Windsor Road as it appeared in the 1950s. Seen amongst some of its numerous traders of the time are Arthur J. Jenkins (gents' outfitter), Ronald Knight (greengrocer), W.H. and B.W. Lawley (newsagents), a branch of the Abersychan & Pontypool Co-operative Society, Chalmers (chemists) and Parton's for fish and chips.

65./66. The origins of Broad Street date from the latter half of the 19th century when in 1866, pioneer Henry Griffiths, with the aid of some local businessmen and shareholders, formed the 'Pontypool Road Benefit Building Society'. The first plot of land purchased by the society extended from Coed-y-Gric Road to High Street, known initially as Cross Street and from Picton Street to the Monmouthshire Canal, including a stretch from Bridge Street to almost the end of Commercial Street where 'Holiday Terrace' terminated. It was on this area of land that streets such as Broad Street, Picton Street, High Street and Bridge Street were formed. The picture above is viewed looking towards the Hanbury Hotel and Windsor Road, while below, from a similar spot but facing in the opposite direction, the buildings forming part of Coed-y-Gric Institute are seen in the background.

67. The cameraman seems to have caused plenty of interest amongst some of Griffithstown's younger inhabitants when photographing Florence Place at the corner with Kemys Street. On the left-hand side and at the far end of the houses, it may be observed that construction work is in progress, the street yet to be completed. The year of this cameraman's work is 1907.

68. Moving a little further up Kemys Street towards St. Hilda's Church and another side street, Grove Place is pictured in 1906 and it too awaits completion on the far left-hand side. Located on an early 1880's map of the village, the first houses to be constructed were those on the nearest left seen with their slate-covered façades but without the apparent need of a pavement.

69. Again, a photographer of almost one hundred years ago has provided this scene at the entrance to Oxford Street with a small group of onlookers gathered outside the Congregational Church which dates from 1885. Oxford Street was originally known as John Street, during which time certain sections of the thoroughfare as with other parts of Griffithstown, were constructed with the aid of the Pontypool Road Benefit Building Society.

70. Back to a busy Windsor Road in the early 1920s where meat purveyors Bach & Son, who were previously established in High Street, are now situated adjacent to Barclays Bank. One door further on and the presence of a photographer has attracted some of the staff from the local post office onto the street. Mr. Robert Chapman who was sub-postmaster during this period, and publisher of this picture postcard, is possibly the gentleman stood on the sidewalk.

71. Hill Street during Edwardian times, viewed at the intersection with Oxford Street to the left and Windsor Road opposite. The corner store looks to be the shared premises of boot and shoe specialist K.B. Webb and draper and outfitter Francis Edward Jenkins whose earlier business was conducted from No.66, Commercial Street. This former trading place may be seen on page 47 when in the capable hands of Mr. Arthur Beynon.

72. From the Kemys Street end, a view of Commercial Street in about 1920, long before the traffic-congested roadway of today. The corner shop on the left at No.1 and nowadays a hair stylists, was then the stores of oil dealer Frederick Lewis Jones. Opposite, the two nearest premises, including Edmunds & James, provision merchants at No. 97 have since been converted into flats.

73. Further along Commercial Street and a busy scene from about 1904 during a period when the thoroughfare enjoyed double the amount of traders of the still-developing Windsor Road, before that was to become the principal shopping area. One name amongst the residents of Commercial Street was Henry Griffiths after whom the village acquired its name 'Griffithstown'. Following his retirement, Mr. Griffiths returned to reside at the since-demolished 'St. Dunstans' until his death in 1915 at the respectable age of 90 years.

74. Having moved from a smaller shop next door some years previous, draper Mr. Arthur Beynon stands outside his store at No.66 Commercial Street, Griffithstown in the year 1912. Prior to Mr. Beynon's occupancy, No.66 belonged to Francis Edward Jenkins, he being described as a draper, stationer and sub-postmaster; this was a period when the business incorporated the village post office prior to relocation in Windsor Road. Some years later Mr. Beynon further expanded his business by opening a millinery shop, also in Windsor Road.

75. The shop premises of Mrs. Margaret Lewis at the corner of Commercial Street and High Street, previously pictured during the 1930s in Volume Two of this series of books. As may be seen, the establishment as it looked in about 1956 has been extended considerably on the Commercial Street side and advertisements for cigarettes and tobacco, the likes of which are much sought after by collectors, are hitherto in abundance. Stood either side of the doorway are Mrs. Lewis on the right with her daughter-in-law Mrs. Eileen Lewis opposite.

76. The lower end of Edward Street in the early part of the 20th century as seen from nearby Charles Street. It was during these times that many people in the locality traded their goods from their own front rooms and two such examples were Mrs. Maria Taylor at No.7 and later Mr. James Brown selling confectionery from No.28.

77. Sunnybank Road in 1930 when the local bus service heading for Pontypool passes by St. Mary's Roman Catholic Church which had opened just a few years previously. The church was blessed and formerly opened by Father F.C. Lynch, Rector of St. Alban's Pontypool, to where followers of the faith had been obliged to travel for worship up until this time. St. Mary's first priest in charge was Father Probert who came from Newport to take up the post which he held for thirteen years.

78. The rear of the housing on Sunnybank Road is to the forefront in this expansive view from the year 1915 that overlooks Griffithstown. In the distance, positive evidence of an industrial past may be seen with Wright & Butler's Phoenix Galvanizing Works far left of centre and above the houses, during the heyday of steam, the busy locomotive sheds at Pontypool Road are in sight.

79. Staffordshire Row in the year 1904, it being renamed Stafford Road in later years. This 19th century-built row of houses was originally constructed to house a group of workers who had moved to the district from Baldwin's works in Staffordshire to take up employment at the Pontymoile Lower Mills Works which, at the time, was part of the Baldwin company. During this period, many were lured from various parts of the country on the promise of high wages and a prosperous future available from the industries of Pontypool.

80. Together with Coed-y-Gric Farm and a few other dwellings near to where the Mason's Arms public house now stands, the two ancient cottages nearest, once formed part of a small community dating back to the late 16th or early 17th century, which was more than 250 years before the development of Griffithstown was forthcoming. The cottages are shown here in 1908 alongside the Monmouthshire Canal at Barretts Bridge and were situated where today's Bridge Street car park stands.

81./82. Two alternative views of the Monmouthshire Canal which are separated by almost four decades. The above scene, looking northwards from Barretts Bridge, Coed-y-Gric Road dates from the 1920s. The bridge structure in the background was used for the transportation of coal to the Institute which later became Panteg Hospital, and was by means of a narrow gauge railway line supported by two rolled steel joists. The coal was delivered from the railway sidings adjacent to the canal and originally, before construction of the railway, would have been conveyed by canal barge. The lower picture, looking towards Crown Bridge Sebastopol, involves a struggling boating enthusiast making his way towards Pontymoile basin via Griffithstown in the 1960s.

83. This far-reaching aerial view from the 1950s showing the lower end of Sebastopol is dominated by the works of Richard Thomas & Baldwin. In more recent times however, the Finnish-based Avesta Polarit plant diminished considerably with extensive demolition taking place at the far end in 2001. Total closure was announced and took place in March 2004 with job losses for the remaining 116 employees and the end of more than 100 years of steel manufacture at Panteg.

84. This is a photograph that depicts parts of Griffithstown and Sebastopol in the late 1920s, before subsequent house-building took a stranglehold. To help readers identify the location, Cwrdy Road is situated to the left, below Cwrdy Farm with the blocks of houses on the Avenue in the centre. Should such a image be taken from the same position today, a total transformation would be revealed with the green fields now a well-developed site.

85. Panteg Park, which was opened on June 21st 1924 and presented to the people of the district in memory of Mr. Isaac Butler. It was Mr. Butler who with other partners, was instrumental in the resurgence of Panteg steelworks in the 1880s. Also well-respected in public life, he was appointed in 1911 as High Sheriff of Monmouthshire as well as holding office as Justice of the Peace. The land for the park was donated by Mr. Butler's family whose representative, son Major A.I.R. Butler, also performed the opening ceremony.

86. Amongst the numerous houses that were constructed on the Kemys Fawr Estate by Panteg Urban District Council, was Rowan Crescent, seen here in the 1930s, the road leading to the Ellipse. The estate was acquired by the council for housing development from Mr. Isaac Butler's family in 1918 and 1919.

87. The Highway, New Inn pictured on a day of little activity during the 1930s. To be seen on the immediate right is one of the district's hostelries 'The Upper New Inn', advertising the once highly-acclaimed Phillips Ales of Newport. Nowadays, this popular 'local' is better known as 'The Teazer', its appearance as well as its name having seen a few obvious changes particularly the dangerous-looking entrance leading on to the main road being removed.

88. Travelling back in time and a short distance further on up the road, this is how it all looked almost a hundred years ago. The photograph provides a good opportunity to examine another of New Inn's public houses, 'The Rising Sun' as it originally appeared before major alterations took place some years later. The gentleman on the left of the picture is standing where these days, the roadway leads to Afon Close.

89. Approximately forty years have elapsed since this view by local photographer Michael Witts was captured on a sunny day along New Inn's Highway. The Teazer public house mentioned previously is visible in the centre, but in more recent years, some major changes to the surroundings have taken place. These include the demolition of the partly-hidden Pineapple Inn (left) and on the opposite side of the road, the garage selling the *Regent* brand of petrol. The ground behind the sign is now occupied by a housing estate.

90. Another scene by the same photographer from a not-too-distant past showing the pre-fabricated bungalows on Lancaster Road. Mass-produced to fill a critical housing shortage following the effects of World War Two, they were intended to have a life span of no more than ten years by which time full scale house-building would have recovered. Known as 'Prefabs', they contained most of the modern facilities for the period and proved to be extremely popular with the occupants, so much so that they often lasted three times their prescribed life and in some areas there were even howls of protest when they were de-commissioned!

91. Once situated at the rear of The Lower New Inn public house, these ancient cottages and blacksmith's shop are pictured during the earliest years of the 20th century. One of the gentlemen in the photograph is thought to be Mr. Llewellyn Lewis who, during this period was the village smithy. The occupation of blacksmith in these early times was a busy and important one, he being in constant demand by both the rural and industrial communities in the area.

92. Back once more to the 1930s to see how the junction with New Road leading to Griffithstown looked then. Facing northwards, a scene from bygone days is to be appreciated, that of the local 'Bobby' possibly on traffic control duty, albeit there is a scarcity of motor vehicles to cause much of a problem, unlike what is found in this part of New Inn almost seventy years on.

93. Part of the railway complex at Pontypool Road station and the surrounding area as seen from an aircraft in about 1930. On the nearside right of the bridge is the old stationmaster's house which dates from the 1850s and still stands to this very day, as does part of a south-facing bay that forms part of the garden of this now private dwelling. To the left of the picture, before being fully developed, is Coed-y-Canddo Road with Hand Farm Road bearing left.

CHAPTER 4

Religion and Schooling

94. The former Bethany Calvinistic Methodist Church and its adjacent Hall that stood for 130 years on St. Luke's Road, Pontnewynydd before eventual destruction at the end of the 20th century. As with many religious causes in years gone by, when followers of a particular faith moved around the country, particularly in search of places to live and work, their beliefs and usually the language went with them. Such was the formation of Bethany, by migrants from distant parts of south and mid Wales whose first language was Welsh, succeeded in attaining their own chapel in Pontnewynydd in 1868, up until which time their nearest venue had been walking distance away at Rehoboth in High Street, Pontypool, itself a demolition victim in about 1970. Services at Bethany were to continue in Welsh until the turn of the 20th century before the English tongue finally took hold.

95. Crane Street Baptist Church which held its first services after opening in April 1847. Formed in the 1830s at the Friends Meeting House in Trosnant, it is one of the few Pontypool chapels to have survived to this day despite it having numerous 'ups and downs' over the years. In 1980 it came very close to total closure through a need of repair and lack of necessary funds but, thanks to the efforts of a band of devoted followers, a rescue package was produced and the situation was saved. More recently in May 2002, a group dedicated itself to safeguarding its future by forming the 'Friends of Crane Street Baptist Church' which hopefully will secure this Grade II Listed Building for posterity. In a 1995 television production, the church was described by Professor Anthony Jones as being the finest of its kind.

96. St. Cadoc's Church Hall and former Sunday School Institute which opened on July 14th 1904 when Rev. Edward Morgan M.A. was the parish priest. Seen above in the 1930s, the Institute was constructed facing the ruins of an ancient barn also used for Sunday School purposes at one time. In more recent times, the neglected hall has been transformed into a Communities First Resource Centre and used to house local groups for community activities, meetings and workshops.

97. Merchants Hill Baptist Church, Pontnewynydd, the origins of which date back to 1874 when a meeting was held at nearby Bethany Presbyterian where it was unanimously decided to form a Baptist Sunday School for children at the earliest opportunity. Prior to this, children and adults were obliged either to walk to Abersychan or Pontypool for their worship. The Sunday School's initial meetings were held in a room known as 'the long room' which was located above the Horseshoe Inn, the only such place available at the time and despite the close proximity of alcoholic beverages, the school flourished under the leadership of Mr. Charles Vaughan its first superintendent. In 1877 a new venue was found when a disused warehouse on Merchants Hill, owned by Mr. Henry Lewis, was offered to the committee who gladly accepted. As the movement grew in number, it became necessary to hold preaching services on Sunday mornings and evenings with the afternoon reserved for pupils of the Sunday School, and so this enthusiasm was to lead to the formation of the first Baptist Church in Pontnewynydd. By 1886 it was decided that a full-time pastor should be appointed and Rev. James Gomer Watts of Glascoed was invited, and accepted to join the Pontnewynydd flock. A new committee was then formed under the chairmanship of Dr. Edwards of Penygarn Baptist College and eventually, a plot of land where an old woollen factory once stood was acquired, with the intention of building a completely new church. This task was completed in 1888, opening its doors for worship on March 18th of that year with services conducted by Dr. Edwards. Still standing today on its original site, Rev. B.J. Morgan currently leads the congregation as he has done since 1994.

98. The Griffiths family, many by marriage, who had long associations with Merchants Hill Church are seen in this 1940s photograph and left to right are - Back: Bert Rule, Ken Rule, Gethin Bishop, Alec Kerr, Don Kerr, Emrys Bishop. Third Row: Rob Kerr (Jnr.), Gwen Kerr, Norman Ball, Olwen Ball, Marion Kerr, Mary Purcell (Jnr.), Kathleen Bishop, Gwen Rule, Seabright Rule. Second Row: Lionel (evacuee), Jim Rule, Arthur Jarvis, Jack Rule, Gethin Griffiths, Robert Kerr (Snr.), William Bishop, Jack Purcell. Seated: Bessie Rule, Annie Jarvis, Martha Rule, David Rule (child), Gertie Griffiths, Gertie Kerr, Blanche Bishop, Mary Purcell (Snr.), Minnie Griffiths.

99. St. Matthew's Church at Blaendare with its distinctive corrugated frontage and gates is featured here during the 1930s. Two of its members from the period are tending the grounds with Mr. Eli Gould on the left (a carpenter by trade) accompanied by Mr. William Harry Crump who is recorded as being an engine driver at Pontypool Road railway complex. The church was dedicated on September 19th 1895 with Bishop Lewis of Llandaff officiating at the morning service and Dr. H.A. James in the evening. Prior to construction of this building, services were conducted at Pontymoile Old School and Panteg Parish Church. From the beginning, the founders regarded the building as but temporary, for, soon after its completion the question of a more permanent stone-built structure was being discussed. As far back as December 1896, Mr. A.A. Williams at a meeting of 'managers' of the church proposed that a quarterly offertory be taken at St. Matthew's in aid of the new church fund. The proposition was seconded by Mr. J.W. Hardon and carried unanimously. The 'temporary' building had cost £450 to construct, of which £400 had been collected well before opening with the remainder forthcoming some 2½ years later. Now, some 110 years on, it still serves its faithful members but sadly, earlier dreams of a more substantial stone-built church never did come to fruition.

100. Some ladies of St. Matthew's pose for a photograph and left to right are - Standing: Mrs. Thomas, Edith Roberts, Mrs. Brown, Grace Gould, Monica George, Mrs. Lee, Mary Stokes, Mrs. Skuse, Ethel Sanders. Seated: Edith Watkins, Mrs. White, Mrs. Gould, Choirmaster Roland (Roly) Pope, Mrs. M. Williams, Mrs. Prosser.

101. A Saint Matthew's Sunday School party at St. James's Hall Pontypool in the 1960s that includes the following, left to right - Back: ?, ?, Margaret Baldwin, Jill Roberts, Jillian Nicholls, Monica George, ?. Middle: Roger Evans, ?, Pat Collins, Heather Jones, Alistair Turberville, Trevor Cole, Anne Davies, David Haggar, ?, Stanley Jones, Lyn Davies, Howard Baldwin, Kenvyn George, Robert Smith, Carol Salt, Sandra Manley. Front: Patricia Evans, Graham and Jill George, ?, John Townsend, Miss Meredith, Judith Nicholls.

102. The above Zion Hill Baptist Chapel, Pontnewynydd opened in September 1881 and was built beside the house of a Mr. James Eyles who had until then, allowed his house to be used for services. As with Merchants Hill Sunday School, described previously, the worshippers of Zion Hill also held their meetings in the 'long room' of the Horseshoe Inn as a temporary measure before their chapel could be built. This chapel survived a long history until finally closing its doors in 2003.

103. This photograph is from St. Oswald's Mission Church, Wern Road, Sebastopol. Workmen belonging to builder H.M. Moseley of Pontypool are outside what was the infants' school whilst in the throes of converting it into St. Oswald's. Substantial alterations to the school, originally built in 1900, began in 1914 with the building of a porch as seen here, followed by a vestry and bell tower. The curate, Rev. Trevor Owen Thomas is the gentleman in the centre and he, with the vicar of St. Hilda's, Rev. H.O. Thomas conducted the service of dedication in March 1915, the dedication itself being performed by the Bishop of Llandaff.

104. Many local residents and those perhaps travelling through Pontypool via Pontymoile cannot have failed to notice the substantial building that used to stand on the corner, that of the Mission Hall which had been a place of non-conformist worship since 1891. Now removed to make way for the sweeping changes that have affected this area, the gathering above provides an opportunity to record and remember some of its members during the 1960s.

105. An impressive view of the interior of Tabernacle Baptist Church, Crane Street with its magnificent pipe organ. Taken in March 1943 when all was well and congregations plentiful, the event is believed to be an annual concert with more than seventy participants involved. The church was built in 1836 with the addition of an adjoining Sunday School in May 1906, then eventually after more than 130 years of ministrations, the town lost yet another historic building in 1970.

106. St. Mary's Church, Panteg has centuries of history behind it and at its doors are members of the choir in about 1977. Included in the picture are left to right - Back: Harold Davies (churchwarden), Mr. Dadge, Mr. Johns, Christopher Hammett, ?, ?, Christopher Baldock, Ted Baldock (churchwarden). Middle: Kim Baker, Elizabeth Evans, Tom Curtis-Morgan (curate), Siân Walters, Mr. Traves, Siân Hutchings. Front: Mr. Jack Lewis (organist and choirmaster), Rachel Rosser, Catherine James, ?, Samantha Williams, Karen Lucket, Joanne Williams, Gaynor Manship, Mr. Payne.

107. A class of twenty-seven pupils, accompanied by two members of staff are assembled at George Street Old School in 1973. Education for local children commenced in this school in the year 1847 and continued as such for more than 140 years before being replaced by more modern premises.

108. In July 1834, Reverend Thomas Davies on his arrival to undertake the curacy at Trevethin, was dismayed to find an old decayed church and a girls' school, that had been set up in a room over Pontypool police station, as the sole means of education in the parish. This state of affairs did not last long, for Rev. Davies soon set about remedying the situation. The Church was fully aware of its responsibilities for educating the young, especially following the principles of the Christian faith and long before any Acts of Parliament came into being, guaranteeing an education for all. In August 1835 the Reverend started a boys' school at the old police station described as the 'Pontypool Charity School' and in later deeds given titles as 'Pontypool Town School' and 'National School'. Thus it was, through his initiative in 1838 that the Town School was built as a church-funded school with accommodation for 300 mixed pupils, and to where masters and their pupils were collectively transferred from various temporary classrooms in the area. The school proved so successful that it was enlarged and improved in 1849 and again in 1896. With the aid of £1,000 endowed by Capel Hanbury Leigh in his Will and other monies from various donors and benefactors, including Reverend Davies who had also bequeathed a sum of £600, the school benefited with extensive alterations in 1904. Educating children of the working classes for well over a hundred years, the school is seen shortly before its demise in the 1970s.

109. The staff of the Town School in a centenary photograph from 1938 and left to right are - Back: Miss M.E. Lewis, Miss G.M. Gameson, Mr. W.D. Howell, Mr. L.V.R. Hughes, Miss M.A. Brooke, Miss S.A. Creese. Seated: Mr. E.F. Rees, Miss R. Long, Mr. J.P. Lewis (Headmaster), Miss E.M. Williams (Headmistress Infants' Dept.), Mr. W.H. Petty.

110. Boy pupils belonging to the New Twmpath Central School pose proudly during the year of the school's opening in 1927. The original school which was sited below Twmpath Hill, was built in 1842 by Capel Hanbury Leigh for his employees' children in the Glyn Valley and at Lower Race. This place of learning educated its pupils for over 80 years from where they were transferred to the aforementioned new premises at the opposite end of Twmpath Hill. Ironically, the old school has outlived its successor, now having been converted into a private dwelling whilst the latter has made way for housing development.

111. A mixed group of staff and pupils are seen in this traditional photograph taken in the yard of Wern School, Sebastopol in the mid-1950s and left to right are - Back: John Jones, Graham Williams, Vernon Prosser, Michael Dibble, Ken Burton, Brian Booth, Ken Asher, Ray Stewart, Alan Bridges, Steven Reed, Tony Davies, Michael Evans, John Woods. Third Row: Margaret Thomas, Yvonne Lewis, Dorothy Price, Gillian Bradley, Joan Carey, Brenda Lee, Gillian Humphreys, Christine Willoughby, Shirley Jones, Kay Hall, Rosemary Andrews. Second Row: Mr. Melvyn Jones (Head), Pat Hall, Rosemary Smith, Pat Rogers, Brenda Doyle, Jean Cogdale, Gillian Fields, Pat Tremlett, Margaret Workman, Mrs. Gulliford. Front: Clive Jeremiah, Tony Harris, John Reed, Michael Bevan.

112. A class of mixed pupils at Cwmffrwdoer Junior School in the 1950s and in the picture are - Back: Graham Howden, Mike Williams, Robert Burns, Tony Roderick, Tony Jones, Brian Beverstock, John Counsell, Jeffrey Pritchard, Russell Foster, Sidney ?. Middle: Marcia Williams, Joan Williams, Sandra Matthews, Janet Winstone, Jane Mitchell, Gwyneth Chattam, Rosemary Martin, Alan Barwell. Front: Unknown, Moira Fitzgerald, Nesta Morgan, Janet Morris, unknown, B.Bonland, unknown, Pat Hillier, Annette Wilson, Janice Palmer, Gillian Chapman.

113. Unfortunately it has not been possible to determine the long list of names of these ladies, however they are members of staff at Pontypool County School for Girls more than likely during the 1950s.

114. A class of twenty-nine children and two teachers are present at Green Lawn School, New Inn, the year being 1975. Unfortunately the author has not been able to trace any names on this occasion but it is very likely that many of those seen in the photograph will now be readers of this book and be able to recognize many familiar faces from the period.

115. Another mixed group from Green Lawn in about 1953-54 and most of the names have been gathered as follows, left to right - Back: ?, Margaret Workman, Margaret Stanley, Marion Webb, Jill Harry, Marcia Hammond. Third Row: Mr. Hayward (Head), Brian Smith, Adrian Leighton, Gareth Moody, Lyn Berryman, Bob Mollaney, Paul Heaton, Terry Ashill, Phil Morgan, John Hampton. Second Row: Jennifer Smith, Barbara Smith, Doreen Cook, ?, Pat Tremlett, Rita Blackmore, Rosemary Smith, Jean Williams, June Powell, Glenys Green. Front: Edward Howe, Paul Evans, ?, Peter Hallows, ?, Michael Griffiths, Howard Pope, Terry Williams.

116. Park Terrace Primary School, Pontypool which officially opened in 1936 and closed its doors in 2001. The original school on this site saw its first lessons conducted in October 1883 with a staff of three teachers and two monitors providing education for an average of 79 pupils, this increasing to 107 after the first year. At its peak, the above building accommodated 170 children, the total having reduced to 116 on the day of closure. Demolition followed in 2003.

117. From 1950 comes this mixed class at Park Terrace and where possible the names are recorded as follows - Back: Mr. Griffiths, ?, ?, Ann Constance, ?, Della Munday, ?, ?, Billy Walker, Bobby Gibbs, Brian Maloney. Middle: Collette Hewitt, Jean Horton, Terry Hallett, Gerald Perry, Michael Smith, Ann Gittings, ?, Valerie Garbutt, ?, Ann Coombs, Terry Pearce, Ken Blake, Miss Beech. Front: Master Price, ?, Sandra Sullivan, ?, ?, Janet Clayton, Ann Lucas, Brian Jenkins, Derek Jeffries, Graham Young, Audrey Cook, ?, John Jeremiah, Tony Morgan, ?.

118. From the pre-comprehensive days at West Mon Grammar School comes this 1959 photograph of the school prefects with - Back: A. Waring, J. Lippiatt, J. Bird, J. Owen, R. Morgan, B. Browning, I. Rowles, J. Gilford. 2nd Row: D. Quick, H. Gabe, P. Davies, J. Troughton, R. Highnam, A. Robertshaw, J. Lucas, A. Rees. Kneeling: J. Claughan, J. James, J. Rosser, P. Ivory, L. Barrell, B. Timms, G.S. Hughes, A. Hodge, R. Simmonds, P. Whittal-Williams. The two other prefects at the time, but absent for the photograph were B. Foster and J. Griffiths.

119. The former village school at Mamhilad, a Grade II Listed Building and one of the few nineteenth-century one-time educational establishments still standing today. With the date of 1856 inscribed above the entrance and constructed for the accommodation of 87 children, its usage as a school terminated in the 1950s. For many years thereafter, the two schoolrooms were utilized as a parish hall by the local church and for a short period as a joinery workshop by Pontypool Park Estate.

120. The date is June 1963 and the third year pupils with their teacher are from Griffithstown Junior School. Looking left to right are - Back: Miss Watkins, Adrian Morgan, Stephen Warrilow, Idris Holloway, Gwyn Davies, Brian Smith, Gareth Marks, Richard Lawton, Terry Wall, Max Chesterman, Andrew Coleman, Christopher Ward. Middle: Stephen Smith, Jayne Thomas, Christine ?, Beverley Howells, Pamela Bryant, Susan Davies, Kay Francis, Elizabeth Williams, Janet Williams, Ann Hughes, Jayne Thatcher, Ian Price. Front: Valerie Hearn, Helen Booth, Carol ?, Yvonne Jeune, Susan Cogdell, Laura Hurst, Ann Morgan, Heather Langdon, Meryl ?, Carol ?.

121. Lads from Pontymoile and Griffithstown schools together during a holiday that was provided free of charge to children during the Depression years of the 1930s. This particular group is seen at the boys camp Gileston, near St. Athan, South Glamorgan and left to right includes - Back: Member of Camp Staff, Teacher Mr. C.O. John, R. Saunders, R. Wall, R. Powell, J. Williams, T. Rowlands, R. Morgan, J. Thomas, Camp Staff. Third Row: W. Bevan, G. Fisher, D. Gibbons, R. Jones, D. Charles, D. Veysey, ?, T. Griffin, D. Day, Teacher Mr. Vaughan. Second Row: J. Turberville, J. Wells, G. Thomas, K. Jenkins, R. Virgin, E. Jeremiah, J. Attfield, G. Norman. Front: O. Evans, D. Jones, H. Williams, A. Phillips, L. Chick, G. Reynolds.

122. It's all smiles from this group of children and their teacher at Snatchwood School, Pontnewynydd around 1952/53 and to be seen are - Back: Robin Layton, Melvyn Pullin, Brian Jobbins, Clive Furnell, Glyn Powell, John Long, Eric Oram, Desmond Kendall, John Price. Middle: Mrs. Childs (Teacher), Douglas Edmonds, Marjorie Drinkwater, Faye Dando, Ann Burke, Terry Evans. Front: Muriel Simmonds, Betty Simpson, Jillian Wall, Brenda Phillips, Ann Redman, Pauline Horseman, Christine Hassel, Pat Martin, Betty Roberts, Wendy Keyes.

123. A party of young lads from West Monmouth Grammar School who were about to set off for an Offa's Dyke walk in about 1980 (a short period before the changeover to comprehensive education). Unfortunately only one of the group's name is known to the author, that being Martin Fawke who is on the extreme left of the front row.

CHAPTER 5

Local People and Events

124. A scene from the turn of the twentieth century facing south and looking down Osborne Road towards Pontypool town centre. The occasion for this lengthy procession that has an enthusiastic following can only be conjecture, but with attendance such as the fire brigade at the helm followed by what appears to be a military band and other military personnel, the event obviously bore some significance during a day in the Edwardian era.

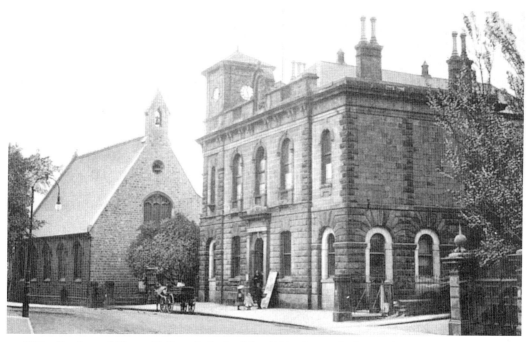

125. Pontypool Town Hall as it looked in 1905. Opened almost fifty years earlier in 1856, this stately-looking building was donated to the town by Capel Hanbury-Leigh in celebration of the birth of his son and heir John Capel Hanbury who was born on 14th May 1853. Capel Hanbury-Leigh was the great-grandson of Major John Hanbury who developed the iron industry in Pontypool's early days. He assumed the name and arms of Leigh in 1797 by right of descent and was also appointed Lord Lieutenant of the County and in the same year married his first wife Molly Anne Mackworth of Neath. After 53 years of marriage she died in 1846 and just over a year later the Lord Lieutenant took a second wife, Emma Elizabeth Rous of Cwrt-yr-Ala, Glamorganshire. Out of this marriage came two daughters Emma and Frances who were succeeded by a third child, the son and heir from a proud father who was now 76 years of age.

Great rejoicing and celebrations followed and to further commemorate the birth, Capel Hanbury-Leigh made a promise to finance the building of a town hall for Pontypool, and thus it was decided that a national competition should be held to design an Italian-styled structure which attracted thirty-nine entries. Hanbury-Leigh himself chose the winning entry from a short list of three, Messrs Bidlake and Lovett of Wolverhampton being the eventual winners and on the first anniversary of the child's birth the Lord Lieutenant and his Lady were escorted from Park House by the Pontymoile Brass Band to lay the foundation stone.

The building contract was awarded to Mr. William Prosser of Abergavenny and the stone used in the construction is said to have been quarried from the Mynydd Maen Mountain above Upper Race. The official opening took place on 1st January 1856, which was followed by a 'grand evening concert' held in the hall attended by 400 people. Such was the importance of this new addition to Pontypool's standing, that further celebrations took place some three weeks later with a grandiose ball being held there with over a hundred specially selected guests in attendance.

126. Carnival Days are always guaranteed to attract large crowds onto the streets and this event from the 1970s is no exception. In this instance perhaps some readers will be able to recognize a face or two in amongst the many onlookers outside the town hall and library.

127. One feature of Pontypool's carnivals in past years was its character bands and jazz bands. The character band movement originated in 1926, the year of the General Strike with its main idea being to give the unemployed an added interest in life and to assist in keeping them active in some way. In 1938 the Welsh National Carnival Bands Association organized the first national championship character band contest in Pontypool Park, when almost 14,000 people watched the event, a long one indeed, it starting at 1.00pm and continuing for more than 8 hours. Above, is the Pontypool Lieutenants Jazz Band parading outside the Clarence Hotel, possibly during the early 1950s.

128. Pontypool Carnival Fête in the year 1950 and excluding the gentleman with the camera, the line-up includes on the left local band leader Eddie Craig who originally came from the United States where he played in the Fletcher Henderson Orchestra during the 'big band era'. Eddie remained in this country after World War Two and settled in Griffithstown after marrying a local girl. Next to Eddie with the flowers is guest artiste, singer Rose Murphy who also hailed from the U.S.A. whilst next to her is the Carnival Queen who stands alongside chairman of Pontypool U.D.C. Mr. Lothian Lewis and his wife. The two gentlemen at the rear are Laurie Denize and Coldridge Goode, both accompanists to Rose Murphy.

129. A considerable crowd of spectators line the route into Pontypool Park as a carnival procession passes by the former lodge at Pontymoile gates. A traditional float, the centrepiece of the picture is seen in about 1936, a period when the customary carnival practice was at its peak. The event seen here came more than 35 years after the first carnival in Pontypool was organized to celebrate the relief of Mafeking during the Boer War in South Africa.

130. A large gathering of Pontypool Post Office staff and their families for the annual Christmas party held at the Settlement in Rockhill Road in about 1954. Included amongst the many partygoers is postman Llewellyn Barwell whose children Pam, Adrian, Alan and Hugh are also present and unfortunately these are the only names that have been made known to the author prior to publication.

131. The investiture in 1969 of the Prince of Wales at Caernarvon was an occasion for street celebrations throughout the principality and the above group from Bridge Street, Griffithstown was one of many. Some of the names known, reading left to right are - Seated: Mrs. Morgan, Mrs. Pearce, ?, ?,. Standing centre: Mrs. Annie Howells, ?, Mrs. Meacham, Janet Watkins, Mrs. Lewis, Mrs. M. Howells, ?. Back: Mrs. Pat Pearce, Mrs. Davies, Cyril Irving, ?, ?, ?, Mrs. Lewis.

132. Some more 1969 investiture celebrations, this time at School View, Pontymoile. Standing are: Gordon Wall, Mrs. Hunt, Beryl Williams, ?, Dorothy and Margaret Baglow, Mary Bailey, Gill Jones, Mrs. Rosser and son, Mrs. Jackson and Michael, Dorothy Pritchard, Don Jones, Mrs. Archie Jones, Gladys Saunders, Mr. Archie Jones and Glyn Reece. Seated: Philippa Reece, Linda Bailey, Helen Jones, ?, Debbie Stokes, Denise Bailey, Paul Williams, Mark Williams, Peter Jackson, Catherine Bailey, the Attfield family, Alyson Jones, Gaynor Jones, Brenda Jones, Susan Jackson and Catherine Knutson.

133. Coronation Day for our present queen occurred on June 2nd 1953 and this celebratory party took place at Gloster Parade, New Inn and amongst the crowd are some names to recall. On the immediate left is a young Dilys Evans, behind Dilys is Mrs. Strutt and next to her is bridesmaid Yvonne Herbert. Holding hands with Ann Smith (the queen) is Michael Jones; Nurse Phillips and Ann Williams stand next to Norman Smith; Vera Horrell and Glenys Green are two of the girls on the right and the gentleman in the doorway is Mr. Bridgeman.

134. A party of almost fifty staff from the Pontypool Woolworth store who, with manager Mr. Gallender seated in the centre of the front row, are pictured at the Clarence Hotel in 1950 for their annual dinner and dance. There are certainly a few recognisable faces amongst the crowd who will be known to a number of readers.

135. A party of St. Mary's Panteg Cubs congregate outside Crane Street station on Remembrance Sunday in about 1960 and amongst the group are Mrs. James, Peter Powell, Robert James, Stephen Goodland, Trevor Cole, Ian Tweedle and Master R. Rice. When this picture was taken the station was fast approaching its closure date with passenger services on the Eastern Valley line ceasing on 30th April 1962.

136. Members of St. James's church are to the forefront in this annual Armistice Day service at the Park Memorial Gates opposite Pontypool Town Hall. Behind the 'No Waiting' sign in the background, the town hall displays an information board by the Urban District Council Road Safety Committee, indicating the number of road accidents in the area. For the interested reader, 7 serious and 13 slight injuries are recorded for the month of September, the photograph originating from the 1960s.

137. From the year 1913 a remarkable photograph of a carnival procession as it makes its way around Clarence Corner and heads towards the park gate entrance at Pontymoile. Also of note is a dray delivery wagon left of the picture and opposite, the Clarence coal depot for Wernhill Colliery which advertises its other depot at Crane Street. The single-storey building on the bend is where Mr. Arthur Jenkins started his cycle business in 1911 as mentioned in Chapter One, page 26.

138. Twenty-three smartly-dressed gentlemen at the outset of a Cwmynyscoy Library outing in 1937 and their names are as follows - Back: J. Pullman, E. Wardale, H. Manley, C. Morgan, G. Hale, D. Morgan, B. Gibbs, H. Curzon. Centre: I. Parsons, T. Arthur, C. Larcombe, J. Cooper, W. Mallett, C. Saunders, W. Arthur Snr., W. Larcombe. Seated: J. Evans, S. Hitchin, T. Evans (Chairman), J. Price (Sec.), W. Arthur Jnr. (Treasurer), R. Manley and E. Long.

139. A crowd of locals from the Bridge-End Inn, Cwmffrwdoer ready to set off on a trip in 1922. The group was known as 'Shoppo's Outing Club' - the name having derived from landlord Bob Jones's nickname. Some names have been traced as follows - Bert Allan, Chris Herbert, Tim Jones, Tom West and Jack Price (Vinegar).

140. Upper George Street, Pontypool as seen prior to the demolition of the three properties right of picture. In the right foreground at the junction with Conway Road, once stood Plasmont House where, during May 1939 a violent murder took place. The house which stood in its own grounds and contained about ten bedrooms was the home of 59 year-old Mr. William Alfred Lewis, a bachelor and wealthy businessman who owned many houses and other properties including shops in the Pontypool district. Mr. Lewis who was described as being a quiet shy man, was found dead in his bed with severe head wounds and a pillow covering his face, it being established that he had died of shock as a result of his injuries.

It was thought at first that the motive had been robbery as Mr. Lewis's bedroom had been ransacked, but a tin box containing £100 was found under the bed only a matter of inches from his body thus casting doubt as to whether any money had been taken at all. Later, it was believed that the murder weapon was a shoe that was worn by the assailant but despite appeals by the police, which included one displayed on the town's cinema screens, no such weapon was ever found. Detectives from Scotland Yard were called to the scene who put forward the theories that either Mr. Lewis had met someone as he walked home from a local school after having been fitted for a gas mask in anticipation of impending war, or that the murderer was already laying in wait at the house, awaiting his return; the deceased had been found the following day by a neighbour and a builder who had been working on the outside. Major and lengthy enquiries were conducted, and the grounds of Plasmont House were searched, re-searched and excavated in the hope of clues that would lead to the killer. All of this was to prove completely fruitless however, and regrettably, the case could only be added to the police files of 'Murders - Unsolved'; Mr. Lewis was buried on Whit Monday 1939 taking the dark secret of an unknown killer to his grave.

141. Garnwen Farm, Trevethin where in 1909 a shocking and callous shooting took place. The victim was a Mrs. Cecilia Harris, a 59 year-old widow who lived alone at the farm that she had run with her husband until he died four years previously. It was on the night of February 20th when Mrs. Harris heard someone creeping about outside the farmhouse and opened the door to investigate. There she spotted Mr. John Edmunds, a miner from Garndiffaith whom she knew and who was walking through the yard carrying a shotgun under his arm. Seeing the intruder, Mrs. Harris shouted at him to go away to which Edmunds answered by aiming the gun at her. As it failed to fire, Mrs. Harris ran back into the house locking the door behind her and made her way upstairs to hide. Meanwhile the assailant smashed his way in and the lady quickly ran back down the stairs making an exit through another door. As she ran across the yard in a bid to escape, Edmunds again aimed the gun which this time fired a shot, hitting the poor woman in the cheek and knocking her to the floor. Lying helpless on the ground, Edmunds then indecently assaulted her and only after pleading with him to remember his own mother did he stop. At this point he proceeded to drag the already severely injured Mrs. Harris inside the house demanding to know where she had hidden any money and whilst searching for this, John Edmunds then grabbed a kitchen knife and cut the helpless widow's throat. Leaving her in a pool of blood, he made off with a mere 5/6d (27$\frac{1}{2}$p) and a watch that had belonged to her deceased husband.

Despite the now-serious injuries, Mrs. Harris managed to haul herself to the nearest farmhouse where she found no-one at home but did find the strength to continue on to the next one which was named 'Penyrheol' where Mr. William Rees and his family lived. Mr. Rees who was at home with his wife and daughter, heard a banging at the door and on opening it, found Mrs. Harris covered from head to foot in blood. Realising that she could possibly die at any moment, a quick-thinking Mr. Rees swiftly handed her pencil and paper so she could write down her claims of having been attacked and robbed by John Edmunds and probably protecting his own innocence of any involvement in the crime, bearing in mind that fingerprint identification by the police was still in its infancy.

Later, Edmunds was found and arrested on charges of the shooting, assault and robbery of Mrs. Cecilia Harris who survived long enough to testify against him. Unfortunately she died on May 5th, more than ten weeks after the incident and before the case could be brought before Monmouth Assizes where other witnesses who had seen the accused at the scene of the crime, had since come forward. The charge against him had by now been changed to one of murder and the accused was duly convicted and sentenced to death. However, on a point of law, an appeal was lodged, claiming that Mrs. Harris had in fact died of heart and kidney problems and not directly as a result of her injuries. This appeal was soon dismissed and John Edmunds, who did not make a final confession, was hanged at Usk prison on Saturday 3rd July 1909. Sometime after the execution had taken place, a double-barrelled gun with one chamber still loaded was discovered in a duck pond near Garnwen Farm by three young men after which, the police expressed much satisfaction that the murder weapon had been found.

142. The scene outside Usk prison in July 1909 on what is believed to be the day when John Edmunds went to the gallows. Many hundreds of people made the journey to Usk that day to mark the punishment and conclusion of an episode in Pontypool's history in what was to become known as 'The Lasgarn Outrage'.

143. This view was taken from Pontypool Park during the Royal National Eisteddfod Week of 1924. Lining the approach road to the park ring from the town bridge entrance, some familiar names advertise their publications amongst which are the South Wales Argus, Echo and Western Mail. Also available to the public is an enquiry office for the London, Midland and Scottish Railway an important and chief mode of transport around the country at the time.

144. The evening of Thursday 23rd July 1868 will long be remembered in the annals of Pontypool when nine lives were lost by drowning at the Glyn Pond in the Cwm Glyn Valley, when what began as a pleasure trip, ended in disaster. As a party of thirteen were returning to the shore, their open boat struck one of the stakes at the bottom of the pond making a hole in the side through which water flooded in. One of the group then jumped out to lighten the boat but as he did so, it filled and capsized. The boat-keeper, Mr. Luke Sanger whose cottage was close to the side of the pond, approached in a punt accompanied by bystander Dr. Essex, but those in the water anxiously grabbed the punt and in so doing, upset that as well. Mr. Sanger went down and failed to re-surface, presumably trapped beneath the iron-built punt.

145. The 2nd Monmouthshire Regimental Band who are outside Park House in May 1915 during the First World War period. The regiment was formed at Pontypool by Mr. R.B. Roden in December 1858 as the 2nd Monmouthshire Rifle Volunteer Corps. Early in the following year further companies were raised at Abersychan, Abercarn, Sirhowy, plus two at Ebbw Vale. These five corps were consolidated with that at Pontypool to form a battalion whose headquarter offices were established at Bank Chambers, Osborne Road. Its recruiting office may be seen in picture 2 of this book. The regimental motto 'Gwell angau na gwarth' (Rather death than dishonour) was composed in 1864 by Lady Llanover, wife of the then Lord Lieutenant of the County.

146. Another military band in the year 1907 during a march through Commercial Street, Griffithstown. Although the occasion is not known, the band has been identified as that of the Royal Field Artillery (Panteg Battery), part of the 4th R.F.A. Welsh Division.

147. On May 10th 1963 the visit by Her Majesty The Queen and The Duke of Edinburgh to the Eastern Valley of Monmouthshire caused great excitement in the district. After visiting Abergavenny and Crickhowell, the entourage arrived at Blaenavon in mid afternoon and, after a short stay, headed towards Pontypool where they were greeted at the Town Hall by Chairman of the Council Mr. Cyril Irving and his wife. This was followed by a visit to the British Nylon Spinners factory at Mamhilad for a short guided tour. The photograph above shows the staff at Pontnewynydd's Western Welsh bus depot waiting for the royal party to pass by and the two gentlemen nearest the camera are Mr. Don Williams and chief inspector Mr. Stan Gough.

148. A Western Welsh Omnibus Company trip to Cheltenham in 1949 by drivers, conductors and friends from the Pontnewynydd depot and among the group are - Mr. Parry and Gordon Levi at the rear. Standing left to right are Lorraine Parry (5th), Roy Emmett, Bryn Watkins, Ken Johns, Ivor Hern, ?, ?, ?, Mrs. Long, C.H. Long, Bridie Williams and Reg Williams. Kneeling in the front row are Doreen West, Mrs. Hern, ?, Marge Watkins, Mrs. Walters, ?, and in the very front is Fred Walters.

CHAPTER 6

Services to the Community

149. Officers and men of the Pontypool Fire Brigade outside their station adjoining the Theatre Royal in Osborne Road around 1912. As early as 1838, Pontypool had its own fire brigade when it was manned by the town's policemen. In 1880 a volunteer brigade was founded by George Augustus Bevan, who was known more popularly as Captain Gus Bevan and following this, over the next 20 years other communities in the valley formed their own local brigades. In 1886 Pontypool's brigade received a new fire engine called the 'John Hanbury' and this particular engine, which was fitted with a steam pump mechanism, remained in use until 1932 when it was replaced by a modern motor-engine vehicle.

150. This early twentieth-century fire brigade photograph shows the Panteg and Griffithstown Division who are displaying a hard-fought-for trophy. Unfortunately just one name has been identified to the author, that of Mr. J.F. Horsel, a native of New Inn who is standing on the far left.

151. More than sixty members of the long-established Pontypool and District St. John Ambulance Brigade are gathered at St. James's Field shortly after the construction of the new ambulance station in 1912. The building, which still survives is at present being used for 'School of Dance' classes.

152. Pontnewynydd St. John Ambulance at Zion Hill Junior School which was their first venue where members met prior to the ambulance hall being opened at Hospital Road in 1938. The division associates proudly display the Hanbury Rose Bowl from their first competition win and left to right are - Back: Mr. Pope, Miss Bessie Pugh, Superintendent Ted Webster, Mrs. Buzzard, Mr. J. Hatchard. Seated: Mrs. Price, Doctor Mulligan, Night Superintendent Mrs. Florence Dukes. Unfortunately the lady on the end has yet to be identified.

153. One of the district's most conspicuous buildings that stood for almost one hundred years was the General Hospital at Pontnewynydd. Built on land donated by John Capel Hanbury, it is seen a few years after its official opening on October 19th 1903, from the newly constructed and purpose-built Hospital Road. This majestic piece of architecture finally lost its battle to remain a fixture in the community in 2001 when it was demolished to make way for proposed housing development, a sad loss of yet another landmark that had adorned the eastern valley for so many years.

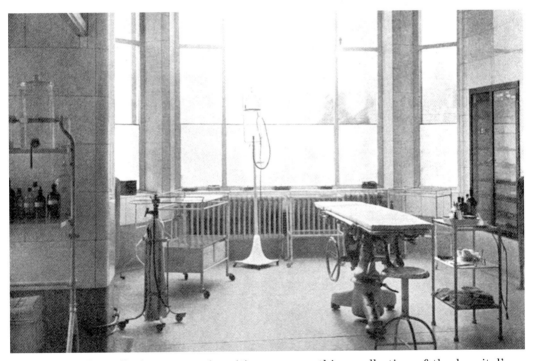

154. For the valley's more senior citizens comes this recollection of the hospital's operating facilities as they appeared in the mid 1930s. Obviously a somewhat antiquated view when compared with what today's theatres have to offer, much successful and appreciated surgery was carried out here in days gone by.

155. The Pontypool Division of the Monmouthshire Constabulary dating from 1938/39 at the rear of Pontypool Town Hall and Police Station and the names given, left to right are as follows - Back: P. Ellaway, C. Mann, E. Moore-Haines, R. Briggs, T. Howells, D. Jenkins, O. Newman, G. Green, S. Parfitt, T. Griffiths, F. Giles. 3rd Row: C. Amett, W. Taylor, unknown, J. Harris, T. Jarvis, A. Conley, F. Graham, W. Ackland, W. Gilbard, C. Wilcox, G. Spencer, S. Bevan, E. Blease. 2nd Row: H. Poulter, J. Harris, E. Clarke, H. Jones, H. Mudway, W. Donoghue, H. Pring, S. Gough, N. Church, F. Keeble, W. Holt, F. Charles, I. Moore, H. Tyler, W. Cross. Front: Sgts. Barry, Bailey, Bowkett, Guy, Bolter and Davidson, Supt. Walbyoff, Sgts. Jones, Morgan, Maggs, Frampton and Constable Barnard.

156. An earlier photograph of some of Pontypool's Police Constabulary dating from around the 1900 period when the force consisted of seven constables and two sergeants under the supervision of Superintendent William James. Just one officer has been identified here however, he being Sergeant Charles Bladon who is seated in the centre of the front row.

157. During the war of 1914-1918 when many of the country's menfolk were away doing their duty, it was the female population that filled the jobs vacated by husbands, brothers and sons, the first occasion ever when women were allocated heavy-duty work previously thought to be reserved for men only. The ladies seen here were from the Pontypool district who, in their Post Office uniforms performed their duties on the home front.

158. With the very real threat of a German invasion during World War Two, a nationwide appeal was broadcast by Mr. Anthony Eden on behalf of the government in May 1940 for civilian volunteers to act as a back-up to the regular forces. Known initially as the Local Defence Volunteers and later as the Home Guard, members of the Pontnewynydd Platoon are outside Pontypool Park House sometime in the 1940s.

159. The Urban District Council of Pontypool ceased to exist on April 1st 1974 following Local Government reorganisation and so one final gathering took place to acknowledge the event with this accompanying photograph. Those present are - Inset: Councillors C Little, G.M. Day, W.R. Bowen, J.L. Whittington and R.T.G. Watkins. Back Row: J.M. Munn (Dir. of Recreation and Leisure), E.A. Keeley (Treasurer), C.R. Evans (Deputy Clerk), W. Brown (Engineer and Surveyor), E.J. Travers (Management Services Officer), J.M. Williams (Chief Public Health Inspector), R.Saunders (Parks and Cemetery Superintendent), T.P. Jones (Housing Manager). Second Row: A.Y. Pitts (Architect), Councillors W.M. George, A. Parry, W. Berry, J.J. Miles, C.J.R. Irving J.P., H.J. Rosser, G.S.R. Powell, C.G. Thomas, D. F.J. Halinan M.B.E. (Medical Officer of Health). Front Row: Councillors Mrs. A.M. Moore, W.L. Jackson M.M., B.E.M., Mrs. M.L. Lee M.B.E., J.P., D.J. Cottrell (Vice Chairman), G.S. Evans J.P. (Chairman), M.B. Mehta (Clerk and Chief Executive Officer), Mrs. M.P. Wells, E.H. Parker, G.I. Miles.

CHAPTER 7

Sports and Pastimes

160. A Panteg cricket team at the club's headquarters during the 1960s. The members include, left to right - Standing: Ian Jones, John Bryant, Richie Thomas, Mike Farr, ?, David Parry-Jones, Peter Barber, Alan Mills. Seated: Barry Morgan, Bruce Davies, Gordon Richards, Ewart Prior. Panteg Cricket Club is a long-established club having celebrated its centenary in 1976.

161. One of Panteg's greatest rivals throughout the years has been Pontnewynydd Cricket Club, pictured here in the mid 1950s, the club being formed originally in 1901. The names are - Standing: Bill Jones, Berwyn Thomas, Alan Bailey, Harry Blackmore, Doug Jolliffe, David Jones, Charlie Jones, Dennis Read, Bill Hopkins. Seated: Redvers Lewis (Jnr.), Jack Lewis, Gwyn Roden, George Peacock, Irving Read, Ken Hewitt, Dennis Haynes. Front: Howard Phillips and Brian Morgan.

162. This photograph from the 1949-50 season features Pontnewynydd A.F.C. Youth XI, two of whom went on to play for the Welsh Youth XI namely Benny Jones and John Larcombe. Back: Jack Fifield, Terry Davies, Jim Rees, Graham Long, Derek Wakefield, Herbert Peploe, Mr. Gough (Trainer). Front: Melvin Jones, John Larcombe, Ken Ball, Benny Jones, Jack Turner, Haydn Taylor.

163. From the year 1957, a group representing Pilkington Bros. Glassworks at tug of war. Back: Tom Williams, Grahame Selby, David Ellis, Roy Evans, Jack Bodenham. Front: Clary Spreadborough, Ivor Nelmes (Coach), Gethin Jones, Ray Williams. Grahame Selby also played rugby for Pontypool R.F.C. as did Jack Bodenham who also played for Newport R.F.C.

164. Players, officials and supporters related to Pontypool Youth Rugby Team are gathered outside Elm House on Park Road prior to the onset of one of their tours in the 1960s and maybe this photograph, will remind those involved of many enjoyable times.

165. The combined Pontypool, Talywain and Blaenavon rugby team who, on December 23rd 1947 at Pontypool Park, narrowly lost by 9 points to 7 to the touring Australian Wallabies; the winning score coming in the closing minutes. In the picture, left to right are - Back: E. Donovan (Touch Judge), Ron Couch, E. Thomas, Wilf Evans, Don Gullick, R. Manfield, Don Hayward, T. Jones (Referee), Tom Rogers. Middle: Sam Lloyd (Trainer), F.E. Davies, Reg Flowers, Ken Norman (Captain), G. Hirst, Ray Cale. Front: Max Horton, Tom Gibbs, A.G. Smith, T. Cooke.

166. One momentous day in the history of Pontypool R.F.C. was the 30th April 1983 when the club won the Schweppes Cup Final, overcoming Welsh champions Swansea by 18 points to 6. Amongst the teams beaten on the way to the final were old adversaries and bogey side Cardiff (13 - 9) and Bridgend who succumbed 19 - 3 in the semi-final played at the Talbot Athletic ground Aberavon. The photograph shows winger Bleddyn Taylor touching down for the only try of the final, ten minutes from the end of the game.

167. A photograph from the 1960s featuring members of Pontypool Judo Club that includes Richie Morgan and Terry Edmunds (standing 1st and 4th left), Barry Evans and Bertreen Griffiths (front 1st left and centre). The club was formed in 1953 by Lyn Irwin and Scot Turner, its first venue being above Morgan's Barber Shop on Osborne Road before moving to a garage at Pontymoile. The next move was to Pontypool Rugby Club gymnasium where Terry Edmunds took charge of the club. The British Nylon Spinners and Crane Street Youth Club were also places where this skilled art was practised.

168. A group of Pontypool Brownie Guides (7-11 Yrs.), a branch of the Girl Guides who on this occasion are believed to have mixed with another of the district's companies in about 1950. Some names have been traced and they are as follows, from the left - Back: Joan Sefton, ?, Christine Allcock, Marie Simons, ?, ?, ?, Mary Bowles, Ann Morgan, Rosemary Powell. Front: Beryl Davies (6th left), ?, Ruby Biggs, ?, ?, ?, Ann Bowles, Barbara Evans, Ann Packwood, Ann Thomas.

169. Another party of Brownies, this time from Griffithstown whose meeting place was at the now-demolished Commercial Street Wesleyan Chapel. On this occasion however, they are pictured at the local junior schoolroom in about 1960-61.

170. The Pontypool Girls' Youth Choir was formed in 1954 by Dorothy Adams-Jeremiah the county music organiser, in close association with Jean Adams, music mistress of Twmpath Secondary Modern School. Members of the choir were past and present students of Twmpath, Abersychan and Sebastopol Secondary Modern Schools and during their time, became a formidable vocal team. The choir is seen at Twmpath School a few years after its formation with Dorothy Adams-Jeremiah seated in the centre, front row and Jean Adams at the piano.

171. This photograph of the Pontypool Girls' Choir was taken at Newport Station at the onset of their trip to Germany on 20th August 1957 where their concert tour included such venues as Cologne, Bonn and Dusseldorf. Dorothy Adams-Jeremiah who led the party is stood in the centre wearing the striped dress.

172. The British Nylon Spinners choir formed in 1951, outside the building known as the Old Welfare Travellers Association which was used as a club house prior to construction of the new and larger premises that were to become a hugely popular events venue. This picture dates from the 1950s and some of the choir members who have been recognized are - Standing: Glyn ?, Mervyn Davies, Francis Walker, John Rodd, ?, ?, Mary Baxter, ?, Kathleen Hobbs, ?, Glen Price, Milton Forward, Martin Baird, ?, Geoff Tudor. Seated: Dorothy Haines, Joan Baird, Elaine Allen, ?, Peggy Beese, ?, Mr. Pinder, ?, ?, Maureen Walters, Audrey Walky, Christine Craxford, Maureen Forward.

173. From the mid-1950s the renowned 'Pontypool Lieutenants Jazz Band', whose meeting place was at the Fountain Inn, Upper George Street, Pontypool, a short distance away from where they practised their skills at the Recreation Ground on Conway Road. This professional group who played in many competitions during their existence, were forced to disband sometime in the 1960s when the Royal Navy disallowed the wearing of their uniforms and badges which they had purchased some years previously with good intent from ex-naval stock. Unfortunately lack of funds prevented the band ever being able to afford complete replacement of outfits.

174. Another, but much younger group of players, the Under 12s 'Malthouse Lane Jazz Band' who are seen here in about 1936. The dedicated and enthusiastic blend of boys and girls met on a twice-weekly basis and were regular contestants at numerous competitions. The more highly skilled members of the party would eventually go on to play in the previously described 'Lieutenants Band'.

The Railway Scene

175./176. Dating from the late 1920s or early 1930s, this group of Great Western Railway workers is stood outside the office entrance of Pontypool Crane Street station goods shed. The busy depot was an integral part of the station's complex and was situated on the site of what is today the town's top car park adjoining the new Tesco supermarket. The view below was taken from a stationary passenger train heading up the valley towards Blaenavon. As will be seen, the shed in later years had been considerably altered and at the time of this British Railways image, contained a number of delivery vehicles which were regularly seen delivering goods around the district. What used to be a hive of activity in this part of town, came to an abrupt end with the yard's closure on October 31st 1966.

177. Pontypool Road, Associated Society of Locomotive Engineers and Firemen (ASLEF) committee and branch members assemble at the rear of Griffithstown Labour Hall during the 1955 ASLEF locomens' strike. The cause of the strike, which lasted seventeen days, was wage differentials and was vigorously opposed by the government of the day, the press, British Transport Commission and even the National Union of Railwaymen. ASLEF members had seen and experienced the principle of such differentials gradually being whittled away ever since the setting up of the Railway Executive in 1948. The Society's claim, which firmly re-established these differentials was presented to the Railway Staff National Tribunal, but their decision, which effectively ignored their case, was rejected by the executive committee. Supported by the entire membership, the strike originally planned for May 1st eventually commenced on the 28th after the Society's continued negotiations for peace bore no fruit. A number of meetings took place before and during the stoppage, when finally, the Commission conceded to the demands made and what had been the longest strike in the Society's history came to an end on June 14th. The settlement figures were not large at 1/6d (7½p) for the drivers and nothing for the firemen, but ASLEF had won the day on matters of principle as they had originally intended.

178. During the 1955 dispute, Pontypool Road ASLEF branch officials importantly kept in touch with district union members from other major areas such as Crewe, Birmingham, Cardiff and Shrewsbury but during that period there was a distinct lack of telephones for such matters. This was overcome by an organized party of motorcycle despatch riders who also conveyed strikers and necessary refreshments to various picket locations. Photographed outside their headquarters (the Labour Hall) in Victoria Street, Griffithstown are some riders and Union officials. The riders left to right are - ?, Fred Smith, Haydn Roberts, Gregor MacMail, Gwyn Hewlett, ?, Albert Stopgate and Charlie Reynolds. Standing: Bill Canning, ?, Arthur Trumper; Tommy Tamplin. Seated: Tom Davies, Ernie Jones and Bill Baker.

179. The abandoned Branches Fork locomotive shed at Pontnewynydd over ten years after its closure in January 1952. Five years previously in 1947, the single-road shed and sub-depot of Pontypool Road had an allocation of two 0-6-0 pannier tank engines, and at the time of this photograph its yard sidings, most of which had by now been removed, still found use as a coal yard until 1969.

180. More railway memories at Pontnewynydd as a Stephenson Locomotive Society Special waits for the all-clear signal to proceed with its journey down the valley to Newport on Sunday May 6th 1962, this was after the official closure of the line to passenger trains the previous week. There were a number of these SLS special outings throughout South Wales providing the enthusiast with a final opportunity to enjoy the nostalgia of steam travel. *(Photo. E.T. Gill)*

181. Trosnant Junction, situated between Blaendare Road Halt and Crane Street station on the Eastern Valley line bearing to the right and where at this point it passed over the Pontypool Road to Neath main line. Pictured in 1967, the signal box for some years had been adapted to enable it to operate the points and signals on the line below. This was carried out in 1933 which then dispensed with the need for Clarence Street signal box, once situated just below to the right. The train from which this photograph was captured heads left on the track that was used for conveyance to and from the collieries in the Cwm Glyn (Crumlin Valley). *(Photo. F.A. Blencowe)*

182. Sebastopol ticket office and halt during its latter days, the office appearing to be standing derelict at the time. The halt opened in 1928 during a period when numerous localities throughout the Great Western Railway were provided with these facilities in order to cut down the walking distances between passengers' nearest stations. Prior to this for instance, Sebastopol residents or visitors would have had a fairly long trek to and from Panteg and Griffithstown to catch a train.

183. The central building in this view which includes Panteg Works and a stationary passenger train, is the old Great Western goods shed dating from 1879 and nowadays the site of Griffithstown Railway Museum. The old building which had stood derelict for a number of years has now been given a new lease of life through the dedication of Mr. Martin Fay, who, with a little help of a few friends and enthusiasts has completely transformed the structure into a museum of railway relics for present and future generations to be proud of.

184. Another building from the railway era still standing, albeit in a dilapidated condition, is the original Panteg Junction station built on the Pontypool Road to Newport (Maindee) lower line. Dating from the 1870s, the station's lifespan for passenger service was rather short which was due to a misjudgement by the GWR in allowing the Pontypool, Caerleon and Newport Company to construct a more direct loop line from Panteg Junction to Pontypool Road, thus bypassing the above station. When Panteg's new station, later renamed Panteg and Griffithstown opened in 1879, this then hastened the closure.

185. Some of the many staff employed at Pontypool Road station throughout the years are pictured here around 1949-1950. Some names have been provided such as Fred Holloway (standing 4th from the left) and Doug Jones who is stood on the extreme right. In the front, left to right are Ray Brown, A. Green, Ted Comley and Lance Carr.

186. A total of sixty-five members of the Pontypool Road Mutual Improvement Class, together with engine driver Ernie Brakespear standing on the footplate. The class is assembled in front of a 'Saint' class engine, type 4-6-0 No.2947 'Madrasfield Court' at the loco sheds in about 1918. Improvement classes were held on Sunday mornings for drivers and their firemen and were undertaken to further their knowledge of the engines on which they worked.

187. A lasting recollection of the once-busy industrial scene at Baldwin's Limited, viewed from the former footbridge above the north-bound platform of Panteg and Griffithstown station in about 1910. Today, the only evidence of this historical reminder is the station's booking office, which is now occupied by a builders' merchant and the old goods shed seen in picture 183, but obscured here by the platform crossover bridge.

188. A magnificent early view of the entrance and approach road to the Great Western Railway's Pontypool Road station, shortly after its opening in 1909 and at a time when rail travel was at its height of popularity. The access to and from the station's platforms was by means of a subway and the number of passengers departing provides typical evidence of the amount of usage that this station once enjoyed.

189./190. An interior view of Pontypool Road round shed in 1963 almost a hundred years after its opening and two years before closure in 1965. The round shed was opened in 1865, replacing an earlier but smaller shed near Coed-y-Gric Junction and was the second turntable shed of the GWR. It consisted of twenty stabling and two dead-end roads with an internal through road connected to an eight-track straight shed on the south side built some four years later. During the construction on May 5th 1865 a sudden collapse of part of the shed caused a number of workmen to be buried, killing two and seriously injuring four. At its peak during two world wars, the shed accommodated over 100 engines coded PPRD by the Great Western and later 86G by British Railways. At the turntable is engine driver Mr. Jimmy Watkins and on the right women engine cleaners are seen at the sheds in 1942, in the middle of World War Two.

Industry

191./192. Tirpentwys colliery pithead in the year 1918 with miners about to descend to their place of work. The two colliers at the front have been identified as lamp-blower Bill (London) Walton on the right and his father Mr. Walton Snr. with the lamp opposite. Mr. Walton is thought to have resided at River Terrace, Freeholdland, Pontnewynydd. The view below at Tirpentwys, shows the after-effects of very heavy rainfall and is quite possibly associated with the great storm that did enormous damage throughout the Eastern Valley in May 1931. Besides the damage seen here, the rain that undermined the mountains of colliery waste dumped over the years by unscrupulous coal-owners, was a catastrophe just waiting to happen.

193. Those who knew what life in a mining district was really like, also knew of the agony and sorrow inflicted by a disastrous colliery accident. This experience fell on the people of the Eastern Valley in 1890, when on February 6th the terrible Llanerch explosion claimed 176 lives. The scene above as rescue parties were still at work, was three days after the catastrophe when a large crowd consisting of thousands was taking part in a religious service at the pithead.

194. The locomotive *'Hafodyrynys'* seen whilst operating at the Crumlin Valley's Colliery at Hafodyrynys. The 0-4-0 ST engine was built in 1919 by the Avonside Engine Company Ltd., at their works at Fishponds, Bristol. The loco is pictured here in 1936 with driver John Yemm on the footplate and shunters Alf May and Harry Williams close at hand.

195. Taking a break from their duties are five tradesmen and two trainees that were employed at Hafodyrynys New Mine, the photograph dating from 1957/1958. Sitting at the rear from left to right are Walter Parry (fitter), Joe ? (welder), Melvin George (fitter), Bill Morris and Neville Taylor (carpenters). The two trainees in front are Roy Davies and John Price.

196. Some of the officials from nearby Glyntillery Colliery on a workday in 1973, two years prior to its closure, Glyntillery having merged with Hafodyrynys in September 1959. Left to right are Penry Long (overman), John Price (deputy), Ivor Harris (deputy), Ernie Vaux (fitter) and Mostyn Jayne (overman).

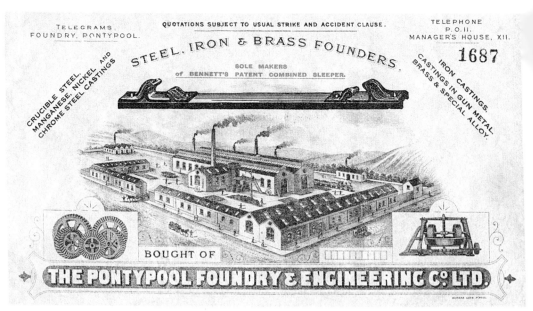

197. A letterhead advertisement promoting the Pontypool Foundry and Engineering Co. Ltd. In 1894 Mr. Thomas Bennett acquired the old foundry at Pontymoile which had previously been established in the early years of the nineteenth century. The firm in 1906, became a limited liability concern and was well known as iron, steel and brass founders. Amongst their products were crucible steel and iron castings for steel works and collieries, besides road gratings, road signs and reflex signs for highway authorities. They were also patentees and manufacturers of 'Bennett's Patent Combined Sleeper and Chair' used for underground haulage roads.

198. The remains of the Race (Blaendare) furnaces as viewed in the closing years of the nineteenth century. Ironworks at Blaendare date back to 1789 when ironmaster David Tanner built two coal-fired blast furnaces. He was also associated with works at Lydbrook, Tintern and Redbrook on the Wye as well as a number of other furnaces and forges in the Pontypool area. In 1799 Mr. Tanner, a native of Monmouth, abandoned all his works and is believed to have left the country for India. On his departure, the Blaendare furnaces were suspended until 1807 when Mr. Watkin George, in conjunction with Mr. Capel Hanbury Leigh restored them, this on the commencement of the tin works at Pontymoile. In its prime, Blaendare was a producer of pig-iron for use at the Lower Mill Works and Osborne Forge.

199. A view facing upstream on the Afon Llwyd, revealing the Mill Weir and Osborne Forge, Pontnewynydd in the year 1907. The name of 'Osborne' appears to have derived from the word 'Osmond' which was a particular type of iron produced at the forge, much of it being for use in the wire industry. The purpose of the weir, a low dam stretching across the river, was to retain the water and regulate its flow.

200. The expansive industrial building in the background of the above photograph belonged to the Lancashire glass company, Pilkington Brothers Ltd. This sheet glass manufacturing plant at Pontypool Road was opened in 1938 in response to a government request to help relieve the stress of unemployment in south Wales. Seen here in the early 1960s, the glass produced at Pontypool was, at the time, largely used for constructional purposes and also sold to safety glass manufacturers for use in the motor industry. Glass was delivered to many parts of the United Kingdom with strong export sales to the Commonwealth and North America. For the railway enthusiast, the locomotive in view is a 2-8-0, 2800 Class, No. 2867.

201./202. An inside look at Panteg works and a group of workmen that operated Numbers 15 and 16 Mills. It is thought that the photograph dates from about 1905, shortly after the tin works had been terminated and converted into a sheet and galvanizing plant. This was a period when labour was being recruited from other industrial areas throughout Wales and the Midlands. The view of the works below, dates from the same decade and was taken from the New Inn side of the main G.W.R. railway line connecting Pontypool Road and Newport.

203. From July 1951 a group of workers from Number 9 Mill, Panteg sheet mills. Unfortunately only three names have come to light and they are Derrick Hall (centre of back row), Jan the Pole (far right back row) and Mr. Manley who is in the middle row, second from the left.

204. A glimpse of Pontnewynydd works in 1962 when the demolition of its two chimney stacks was in progress, bringing an industrial era to an end. The stacks, one 180 feet in height and completed in 1910 and the other at 110 feet, when built took about twelve months to construct and after their days were done, both toppled to the ground in a matter of seconds. At closure in December 1961 only three of the existing twelve mills were still in use, whereas at one time sixteen were operating.

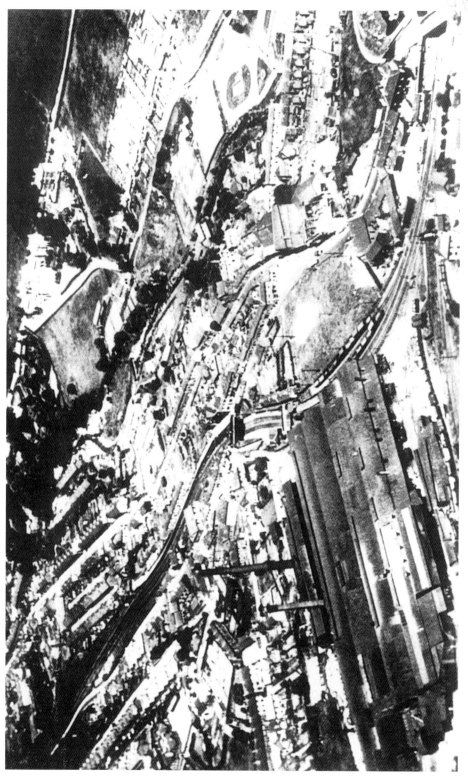

205. Pontnewynydd works when in the hands of Partridge, Jones and John Paton Ltd. is again featured in this 1920's aerial view of the district. Another characteristic of what is today a much-changed scene, is the meandering Eastern Valleys railway line, partly engineered on the path of the former Monmouthshire Canal. Also visible is the abandoned Eastern Valley Brewery; this building stands on the opposite side of the grassed area in front of the works and close to the Horseshoe Hotel.

CHAPTER 10

Pontypool Town Past and Present

206./207. Two photographs that are separated by almost a ninety-year span, both taken from a similar spot in Commercial Street looking towards George Street, the view above appearing to have been on a busy market day. A weekly market was held on a Saturday as early as 1690 for the selling of all manner of cattle, goods and merchandise. In 1730 the old corn market was established and for many years Pontypool was one of Monmouthshire's largest and principal commercial marts. In the upper picture, the site of the old corn market is partly obscured by the overhanging blind, whilst in 2004 a much quieter town is captured. Times have certainly changed here!

208./209. The scene at Crane Street from about 1910 reveals a period of prosperity, when the streets were very active and vacant shops unheard of. Although the town has gone through a few lean decades of late as far as traders and shoppers alike are concerned, the on-going development below will hopefully stimulate both, in that perhaps a more favourable future lies ahead.

210./211. Less than forty years divide these two pictures of Osborne Road and the changes that have occurred contain the structure on the left advertising Bristow and Wadley and of course some household names from the past that are no more. Included in these are Masters (clothier), Johnsons (dry cleaners), J. Winterhalter (jeweller), Melias (grocers), Watson Roden (hairdresser), and Williams Brothers (cycles). More recently, with some premises now standing vacant, it is hoped that the proposed, but much delayed Wetherspoon project will help regenerate the area somewhat closer to previous identities.

212./213. A busy period in Commercial Street in the 1950s when one of its thriving businesses was the central store of the Abersychan and Pontypool Co-operative Society. The former emporium now standing derelict, first opened in 1938 with its last occupant being a branch of 'Hypervalue' who closed the shop almost a decade ago. This 'Art Deco' designed structure pictured below, in 2004, should surely be considered for preservation in some way and not allowed to fall into total disrepair and remain an eyesore for the town!

214./215. Clarence Street, which is another area of the town that has sadly been neglected in recent years, particularly the Clarence Hotel a former showpiece as one passed through Pontypool. Shown above in the late 1930s, when parking was not a problem, the hotel was then a successful and popular venue for both locals and visitors. The more recent photograph however presents a sadder picture but with plans to refurbish this landmark, albeit into flats, (also another delayed scheme) and further ideas for the wider Clarence Corner area, a transformation of appearance can only benefit the town and its residents.

A Message of Appreciation from the Author

I would like to extend my sincere thanks to a number of friends and acquaintances listed below, whose help with the loan of some photographs and accompanying information has been invaluable in the production of this book. If by chance, I have inadvertently omitted anyone, will they please accept my humble apologies.

I particularly wish to pay tribute to my wife Margaret for her continued patience, tolerance and opinions, all of which have played a vital part in the publication of my books over recent years. Also I am indebted to fellow local author Malcolm Thomas for his usual professional guidance and advice throughout.

Mr. Jeffrey Bird, Mr. David Boddington, Mrs. Irene Boulter, Mr. Peter Brookson, Mr. R.S. Carpenter, Mr. Sean Casey, Mr. Howard Cole, Mr. Trevor Cole, Mr. Anthony Crump, Mr. Clive Davies, Mr. Ken Davies, Mr. Johnny Evans, Mr. Roy Evans, Mr. Ernest and Mrs. Brenda Fawke, Mr. Martin Fay, Mr. Kevin Gauntlett, Mr. Gordon Griffiths, Mr. Gwyn Hewlett, Mr. Alan Hodge, Mr. Hubert Howells, Mr. Lyn Irwin, Mr. Brian Jenkins, Mr. Richard Jenkins, Mr. Alan Jones, Mrs. Gill Jones, Mrs. Beverley Lampard, Mrs. Pat Lewis, Mr. Brian J. Miller, Rev. B.J. Morgan, Mr. Martin Pope, Mrs. Marie Price, Mr. John Price, Mr. and Mrs. Doug Pitten, Mrs. Philippa Reece, Mrs. Marge Roberts, Mrs. Pam Robinson, Mrs. Glenys Roynon, Mr. Richard Roynon, Mrs. Gladys Saunders, Mrs. Violet Skillern, Mr. Ray Stewart, Mr. Mike Taylor, the late Mrs. Beryl Thomas, Mr. Gwyn Tilley, Mr. Tommy Tremlett, Mr. Robert and Mrs. Maureen Walters, Mrs. Coral Westcott, the late Mr. H. Williams, Mr. John S. Williams, Mr. Michael Witts.

Additional titles by Bryan Roden

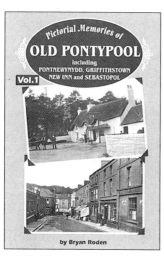

ISBN 1 874538 86 7

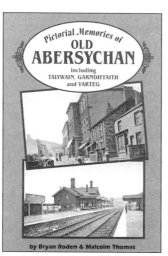

ISBN 1 874538 52 2

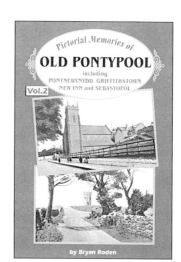

ISBN 1 874538 04 2